HOMELAND SECURITY
OPERATIONAL ANALYSIS CENTER

Forecasting Public Recovery Expenditures' Effect on Construction Prices and the Demand for Construction Labor

AARON STRONG, JEFFREY B. WENGER, ISAAC M. OPPER, DREW M. ANDERSON, KATHRYN A. EDWARDS, KYLE SILER-EVANS, JESSIE COE, R. J. BRIGGS

This research was published in 2022.

About This Report

On October 30, 2017, Puerto Rico elected to participate in alternative procedures for large-project funding for Public Assistance categories C through G, pursuant to Section 428 of the Stafford Act, for permanent work following Hurricane María.[1] In accordance with *Public Assistance Alternative Procedures (Section 428): Guide for Permanent Work* (Federal Emergency Management Agency [FEMA], 2020), the role of the expert panel is to provide an independent validation of cost estimates for Public Assistance projects that are submitted for review.

This report provides FEMA expert guidance in moving forward with future FEMA initiatives specific to the islands of Puerto Rico. In support of this effort, this report provides a suite of estimates in which we have incorporated the effects that the continental U.S. labor supply has on the overall price index. This work was completed in 2019 to provide estimates for the impact on prices in 2020 and beyond. This research was sponsored by FEMA and conducted within the Disaster Research and Analysis Program of the Homeland Security Operational Analysis Center (HSOAC) federally funded research and development center (FFRDC).

About the Homeland Security Operational Analysis Center

The Homeland Security Act of 2002 (Section 305 of Public Law 107-296, as codified at 6 U.S.C. § 185) authorizes the Secretary of Homeland Security, acting through the Under Secretary for Science and Technology, to establish one or more FFRDCs to provide independent analysis of homeland security issues. The RAND Corporation operates HSOAC as an FFRDC for the U.S. Department of Homeland Security (DHS) under contract HSHQDC-16-D-00007.

The HSOAC FFRDC provides the government with independent and objective analyses and advice in core areas important to the department in support of policy development, decisionmaking, alternative approaches, and new ideas on issues of significance. The HSOAC FFRDC also works with and supports other federal, state, local, tribal, and public- and private-sector organizations that make up the homeland security enterprise. The HSOAC FFRDC's research is undertaken by mutual consent with DHS and is organized as a set of discrete tasks. This report presents the results of research and analysis conducted under task orders 70FBR218F00000141, "Expert Analysis of FEMA Cost Estimate Development Process and Validation for FEMA-4339-DR-PR and FEMA-4340-DR-VI (Hurricane Maria) Reme-

---

[1] *Section 428* refers to that section of Public Law 93-288, also known as *the Robert T. Stafford Disaster Relief and Emergency Assistance Act, 1974*, or *the Stafford Act*, as added by Public Law 113-2, 2013, and codified at 42 U.S.C. § 5189f.

diation/Reconstruction," and 70FBR221F00000015, "Future Price Forecast Report Development and Maintenance under DR-4339-PR and DR-4340-VI (Hurricane Maria)."

The results presented in this report do not necessarily reflect official DHS opinion or policy.

For more information on HSOAC, see www.rand.org/hsoac. For more information on this publication, see www.rand.org/t/RRA1116-4.

Acknowledgments

We thank Julia Moline, Maximo Lopez Rodriguez, and Ivya Hernández Cruz of our FEMA sponsor office for their support in facilitating and engaging over the course of this work. Within HSOAC, we thank Jessie Riposo, director of the Disaster Research and Analysis Program, which is the program under which this work was executed. In addition, we benefited from constructive comments from James Hosek, Michael G. Mattock, and Erez Yerushalmi. Finally, we benefited from the research support of Sangita M. Baxi, Kurt Klein, Geoffrey E. Grimm, and Kristin Sereyko.

Summary

Challenge

Hurricanes Irma and María had devastating consequences for Puerto Rico. By the governor of Puerto Rico's estimate in the 2018 recovery plan, approximately $100 billion in investment is necessary to recovery from the damage (Central Office for Recovery, Reconstruction and Resiliency, 2018). With the passage of the Sandy Recovery Improvement Act of 2013 (Pub. L. 113-2, Division B), which added Section 428 to the Stafford Act,[1] the Federal Emergency Management Agency (FEMA) obtained authorization to implement alternative procedures for Public Assistance (PA) funding without notice of rulemaking. Prior to the addition of Section 428, an entity receiving PA funding was required to pay for a project and then be reimbursed by FEMA for reasonable costs with a local cost share. Thus, an entity would need to have funds up front to pay for projects.

Section 428 alternative procedures allow the applicant to bundle projects together and to not build back to the same state as predisaster. Cost overruns are the responsibility of the applicant, and cost savings can be invested in other mitigation and risk reduction activities. In most cases, current construction costs are a good proxy for future costs, accounting for inflation. In the case of Puerto Rico, the scale of the recovery efforts relative to the size of the economy (approximately $110 billion gross domestic product in 2019 [Bureau of Economic Analysis, 2021]) means that the recovery efforts are likely to fundamentally change the economy in terms of labor, materials, and equipment. As a result, in this project, we aimed to develop estimates of future construction costs and build multiplicative factors that cost estimators can apply to current costs to reflect the future cost of construction.

Approach

There were four main components to this work:

- First, the governor's plan does not include an implementation plan. To overcome this, we developed a disaster recovery expenditure simulator based on historical FEMA PA obligations for hurricanes from 1998 to 2017. We incorporated various assumptions about which storms to include and capacity constraints at the beginning that could limit expenditures.

---

[1] *Section 428* refers to that section of Public Law 93-288, also known as *the Robert T. Stafford Disaster Relief and Emergency Assistance Act, 1974*, or *the Stafford Act*, as added by Public Law 113-2, 2013, and codified at 42 U.S.C. § 5189f.

- Second, we developed a computable general equilibrium model to estimate the effect that different expenditure scenarios have on the prices of labor, materials, and equipment in the economy of Puerto Rico.
- To better calibrate the model, we developed an econometric approach to estimate the substitutability of construction and nonconstruction labor that is used to calibrate one of the key parameters in the computable general equilibrium model.
- Finally, the labor force in Puerto Rico might not be able to complete the recovery efforts. To better understand the labor demands necessary, we developed an occupation-level labor demand estimator and compared the labor necessary for the recovery to what was available in Puerto Rico. This provided us with an estimate of the likely need for imported labor in the construction sector because all construction is local.

This work was performed in 2019, so we chose 2020 as the beginning of the reconstruction efforts.

Key Findings

There are three main findings.

First, the labor demands necessary for the recovery efforts are considerably more than what labor is available in Puerto Rico. We estimate that approximately 75 percent of the necessary labor for the efforts will come from sources outside Puerto Rico. Because imported labor is considerably more expensive than local labor, this will be one of the main drivers of cost increases for the recovery efforts.

Second, given Puerto Rico's small, open economy with supply chain connections to the continental United States, as well as international sources, material prices are not likely to increase significantly. We do acknowledge that, at the early stages of the reconstruction efforts, there could be frictions in the supply chain that would increase costs over those in a small, open-economy assumption.

Finally, implementing the estimated future price forecast factors requires an acknowledgment that cost estimators will always use the most-current prices. (The future price forecast is the portion of the increase in price that is due to the demand surge driven by the recovery efforts.) As a result, as time passes, current prices should embody part of the future price forecast. General inflation is addressed in Part E of the Cost Estimating Format, a FEMA tool for determining the cost of permanent work for large construction projects. Thus, monitoring the difference between current prices and estimated future prices is important to avoid double-counting price increases. As current prices increase, future price forecast factors need to decrease commensurately.

Recommendations

The alternative procedures made possible by Section 428 of the Stafford Act make it easier for communities to build back more appropriately to their current situations than standard procedures would have allowed. This comes with both benefits and costs in terms of flexibility of the projects that can be pursued but shifts the risk from FEMA to the applicant in terms of cost overruns. We have identified an instance in which modifications to the 428 process could lead to additional cost overruns that might not fit in the current version of the Cost Estimating Format. Because very little implementation has occurred under these alternative procedures, guidance to applicants about when they are appropriate could be advised. Further, the ability to bundle projects could lead to a slower reconstruction process because these are considerably more-complicated projects than simply building back to prestorm states.

Contents

About This Report iii
Summary v
Figures and Tables xi

CHAPTER ONE
Introduction 1

CHAPTER TWO
Understanding the Labor Supply Constraints for Recovery 5
  Overview of the Steps Involved in the Analysis 6
  Input–Output Model to Estimate Aggregate Demand from Recovery Spending 9
  Translation of Employment Needs to Occupations 10
  Wage Disparity Between Puerto Rico and the Continental United States 14
  Focus on the Construction Industry 16
  Implications 16

CHAPTER THREE
Estimating Expenditure Scenarios 19
  Estimating Yearly Expenditures 19
  Adjustments to the Spending Path to Better Mimic Hurricane María 22

CHAPTER FOUR
The Computable General Equilibrium Model 25
  Model Specification 26

CHAPTER FIVE
Estimating Construction and Nonconstruction Labor Substitutability 31

CHAPTER SIX
Results of the Modeling Approach 37
  Labor 37
  Equipment 39
  Materials 40

CHAPTER SEVEN
Implementation 41
  Choosing a Time Point on the Curve 41
  Operationalizing the Model Results for Each Component 42

A Single Future Price Forecast Factor for Square-Footage Estimates........................46

Implications..48

CHAPTER EIGHT
Discussion and Limitations...49

Abbreviations...53

Bibliography...55

Figures and Tables

Figures

3.1. Obligation Curves for Hurricanes Katrina, Sandy, and All Other Hurricanes 21
3.2. Average Expenditure for Each Assumption, in Billions of Dollars 24
4.1. Production Functions in Each Sector 27
6.1. Estimated Local Average Wages for Public Assistance Projects 38
6.2. Equipment Rental Prices for Public Assistance Projects 39
6.3. Material Prices for Public Assistance Projects 40

Tables

2.1.   Mapping from Courses of Action to Sectors and Cost Proportions 6
2.2.   Aggregate Economic Impact of a $1 Billion Recovery Expenditure in
       Puerto Rico 9
2.3.   Total Effects of Alternative Recovery Expenditures 10
2.4.   Employment, by Industry, for Recovery Expenditures 11
2.5.   Employment, by Occupation, for a $10 Billion Recovery Effort 12
2.6.   The 30 Highest-Demand Employment Positions, by Occupation,
       for a $10 Billion Effort 13
2.7.   Wage Disparity Between Puerto Rico and the United States Generally and
       the Six States with the Most Migration from Puerto Rico 14
2.8.   Construction Employment for a $10 Billion Recovery Effort 17
5.1.   Estimation Results 35
7.1.   Estimated Future Price Forecast Factors for Equipment 42
7.2.   Estimated Future Price Forecasts for Materials 43
7.3.   Estimated Future Price Forecast Factors for Materials 44
7.4.   Estimated Future Price Forecasts for Local Labor 44
7.5.   Future Price Forecasts for Labor 46
7.6.   Gordian Labor City Cost Indexes for Puerto Rico for 2019 46
7.7.   Future Price Forecast Labor Factors for Puerto Rico, by Zone and Year 46
7.8.   City Cost Indexes for Puerto Rico, by Zone and Component, 2019 47
7.9.   Current Cost of Construction, by Zone 47
7.10. Future Costs of Entire Construction 47
7.11. Single-Factor Future Price Forecast Factors for Use with Square-Footage
       Estimates 48

CHAPTER ONE

Introduction

Recovery efforts in Puerto Rico since Hurricanes Irma and María have presented unique challenges with utilizing historical data in cost estimation, especially with respect to construction markets. The comprehensive nature of Puerto Rico reconstruction efforts is unprecedented and therefore has no analogue in relevant historical data. Furthermore, it remains unfeasible to make inferences based on market-sector analysis because the composition across Puerto Rico's industry sectors cannot be predicted in the destabilized economy. Given the anticipated size of the reconstruction efforts in Puerto Rico, it is of paramount importance to understand the time path of construction. If construction expenditures exceed the scale that can be undertaken with current capacity, large price increases will ensue, construction will be delayed, and fewer projects will be completed within the existing budget. In 2017, prior to the hurricanes, the construction sector in Puerto Rico constituted approximately $2.4 billion (IMPLAN, undated) in annual economic activity, representing approximately 2 percent of Puerto Rico's $100 billion economy (Federal Reserve Bank of St. Louis, 2021). The governor's 2018 recovery plan sets out a recovery spending plan of approximately $100 billion in upfront reconstruction costs. A reconstruction effort of $10 billion on average per year for ten years is likely to cause significant economic disruptions and provide large monetary incentives for new labor supply and capital equipment investments, especially given that the population in Puerto Rico has seen significant declines since 2006 (World Bank, 2021).

The Federal Emergency Management Agency (FEMA) is increasingly interested in funding Public Assistance (PA) expenditures via fixed-price grants rather than cost-plus grants. This greatly reduces the administrative burden on both FEMA and local governments while providing local governments more flexibility in how they rebuild. However, fixed-price contracts require accurate forecasts of the cost of the rebuild because under- and overestimates of costs have significant consequences. A systematic bias in cost forecasting that underpredicts costs would subject local governments to financial risk or risk that projects will not be completed because of a lack of funds. Conversely, a systematic bias resulting in overforecasting rebuilding costs would result in the federal government paying millions of dollars more than actual costs. There is currently a buffer in the Cost Estimating Format (CEF) that allows for costs to exceed expectations up to 10 percent. Beyond that, however, a fixed-price contract will underforecast the cost of rebuilding. Therefore, a future price forecast (FPF) is important to understanding how costs will change under recovery expenditure scenarios and is particularly important when the forecast indicates that aggregate costs will increase by more than 10 percent.

In this report, we describe a methodology we developed for estimating the likely impact that the large recovery efforts outlined in the governor's plan will have on Puerto Rico's construction sector, as well as historical PA funding for hurricanes. Our approach was to develop a computable general equilibrium (CGE) model of Puerto Rico's economy. Some parameters and inputs to this modeling effort have previously not been considered in the literature:

- First, because of the size of the recovery efforts and the construction labor force in Puerto Rico, there are likely to be mismatches in those sizes and in skills necessary to complete the recovery efforts. We used an input–output model together with the governor's 2018 recovery plan, as well as U.S. Bureau of Labor Statistics (BLS) occupations by sector (BLS, 2021), to estimate the occupation-level labor demands. Importantly, this analysis allowed us to estimate the share of construction employment likely to come from sources not located in Puerto Rico.
- Second, although the then-governor developed a plan for the efforts, there is no implementation plan. To overcome this, we used historical obligations from PA to develop an expenditure simulation tool to explore a variety of assumptions of how quickly Puerto Rico could ramp up efforts given administrative capacity constraints.
- Third, because we were modeling the construction labor force, we needed to estimate how substitutable construction and nonconstruction labor were as part of the production function for construction. These estimates did not exist in the literature. As a result, we used an approach consistent with that in Katz and Murphy, 1992, with nationwide March Current Population Survey (CPS) Annual Social and Economic Supplement data for 1980 through 2018 (U.S. Census Bureau, undated). These estimates are based on U.S. aggregate wage and employment ratios for the construction and nonconstruction sectors.

Our overall approach was to develop a set of factors that cost estimators could use with FEMA's CEF. We grouped the costs into three broad categories—labor, materials, and equipment—and provide a single estimate based on the average composition of labor, materials, and equipment used in building construction.

With the passage of the Sandy Recovery Improvement Act of 2013, which added Section 428 to the Stafford Act,[1] FEMA obtained authorization to implement alternative procedures for PA funding without notice of rulemaking. Prior to the addition of Section 428, an entity receiving PA funding was required to pay for projects and then be reimbursed by FEMA for reasonable costs with a local cost share. Thus, an entity would need to have funds

---

[1] *Section 428* refers to that section of Public Law 93-288, also known as *the Robert T. Stafford Disaster Relief and Emergency Assistance Act, 1974*, or *the Stafford Act*, as added by Public Law 113-2, 2013, and codified at 42 U.S.C. § 5189f.

up front to pay for a project. In addition, because local and state entities were responsible for only a share of the costs of their projects, their incentive to control costs was reduced: The risk of cost overruns fell disproportionately on FEMA. Finally, reconstruction had to constitute building back to the predisaster state unless there were changes in codes and standards.

With the introduction of Section 428, greater flexibility was granted to recipients such that projects did not need to be rebuilt to previous specifications and, importantly, projects could be bundled together to achieve programmatic goals rather than individual project goals. For example, if four schools were destroyed, three or five schools could be newly constructed in different areas instead of having to rebuild the four, depending on the recipient's needs. Importantly, if a project comes in under budget, those excess funds can be used for mitigation or resilience projects in support of the designed project. This new policy provides incentives to the recipient to be as cost-effective as possible. Finally, applicants have a limited opportunity to renegotiate costs after a project's cost has been estimated. Thus, cost estimates prepared as part of the bid submission are incredibly important because the applicant bears all the risk of cost overruns. The aftermath of a major disaster has the potential to fundamentally change the economy or induce significant price increases because of the demand-side pressures of reconstruction. Generally, project costs are estimated based on current prices for the labor, materials, and equipment necessary for the reconstruction efforts. Engineering estimates for a single project cost do not consider whether the project is part of a larger recovery effort. As a result, simply focusing on project- rather than program-level costs has the potential to significantly underestimate the true cost of construction *when* the construction occurs.

Prediction of future construction costs is essential when projects require funding in advance of task execution and delivery. This is especially true when the scale of project funding is such that it will have economywide impacts. In most cases in which comprehensive estimation efforts are required, cost escalation directly corresponds to predicted future inflation rates. When projects are small compared with the economy or construction sector, a producer price index can be leveraged, and historical data are likely to be an effective estimator of future outcomes. However, when projects are large relative to the size of the economy, future cost projections based on historical producer price indexes will likely be inaccurate. Large projects, or suites of projects, will likely shift both demand and supply to meet the market requirements of new equilibrium conditions. Because market prices are the result of the interaction between supply and demand, general equilibrium models need to be employed to estimate the impact that large-scale efforts can have on prices.

The work we report here was performed in 2019. As a result, the choice of 2019 as the base year is an appropriate choice. This report is meant to document the entire modeling process on which the original estimates were based.

The remainder of this report is organized as follows:

- Chapter Two gives our estimates of the labor demands for recovery efforts.
- Chapter Three provides a method of estimating the recovery expenditure time path across all PA categories.
- Chapter Four provides an overview of the CGE model used to estimate future local prices.
- Chapter Five shows our estimates of the substitutability between construction and non-construction labor.
- Chapter Six provides the results of the entire modeling effort.
- Chapter Seven provides a discussion of how these estimates are implemented in the CEF used by FEMA.
- Chapter Eight provides some additional discussion and caveats of the work.

CHAPTER TWO

Understanding the Labor Supply Constraints for Recovery

Our first step in the analysis was to estimate the labor demands necessary for the recovery efforts. Given Puerto Rico's relative isolation from the rest of the United States, the size of the recovery efforts relative to the size of the economy, and the declining population in Puerto Rico since 2006, the labor force necessary to perform the recovery efforts might not exist. Additionally, the skill mix might not be adequate to perform all of the work necessary, especially with respect to utility reconstruction. These estimates will also help us identify how much labor will be needed from outside Puerto Rico.

We used an input–output model for this estimation because we wanted to have more sectors (536), and we used the BLS occupation-by-industry tables (BLS, 2021) to understand the mix of occupations and not simply the aggregate labor demand. Later in this report, we describe our CGE model with far fewer sectors than those used in the input–output model. Secondarily, this analysis was done to help the U.S. Economic Development Administration develop training programs targeting specific occupations.

Our overall approach was to first translate the governor's 2018 recovery plan into direct spending in different sectors. Next, we built an input–output model calibrated to the economy of Puerto Rico and shocked that model with the increases in demand from the governor's plan. This provided us an increase in sector-level employment, not just for the direct labor but also for the indirect employment coming from intermediate goods and services. Finally, we translated these sector-level employment increases to occupational employment increases using the BLS occupation-by-industry tables (BLS, 2021) and the Occupational Employment Statistics program to understand the training requirements for each occupation.[1]

As previously mentioned, this analysis was originally conducted to support the Economic Development Administration's efforts to develop occupational training programs as part of Puerto Rico recovery efforts. We used it here to understand the occupational and labor force deficiencies in Puerto Rico.

---

[1] Until March 2021, the Occupational Employment Statistics program was the Occupational Employment and Wage Statistics program.

Overview of the Steps Involved in the Analysis

Step 1: Assess the Labor Required for the Recovery Efforts

Our first step in understanding the impacts that recovery spending could have in Puerto Rico was to better understand the labor required for the recovery efforts. Building on the governor of Puerto Rico's 2018 recovery plan, we estimated the expenditures, by sector, with a series of scenarios. We used an input–output model to estimate the plan's impact in terms of output, value added, employment, and labor income. An input–output model is used to compute the *direct effect* of scenarios. Then, the change in sector outputs become inputs into other sectors (*indirect effects*). Finally, these induce expansions of final demand across the economy due to higher incomes (*induced effects*). When combined, these impacts provide an estimate of the scale and composition of new economic activity and how the local economy would react to recovery efforts.

Our modeling approach for this assessment step entailed a four-step process. In the first step, we matched each of the courses of action (COAs) described in the recovery plan to one of four two-digit North American Industry Classification System (NAICS) sector codes (construction, administrative services, management of companies, and educational services), based on keywords in the COA descriptions. Using these keywords as categories, we determined a breakdown of the recovery plan costs based on the cost estimates embedded in the plan. Table 2.1 provides the rough mapping from COA to sector.[2]

TABLE 2.1

Mapping from Courses of Action to Sectors and Cost Proportions

Sector	Keywords in Courses of Action	Plan Cost Percentage
Construction	*Built, build, repair, replace*	48
Administrative services	*Incentivize, plan, study, task force, steering committee*	39
Management of companies	*Business consulting, assist, manage, compensate, improve, implement*	12
Educational services	*Training, schooling, education*	1

SOURCE: The governor's 2018 recovery plan.

---

[2] We have performed sensitivity analysis of the categorization and relative contribution. Importantly, administrative services, management of companies, and educational services have similar economic multiplier impacts, so a misspecification across these three categories is likely not to have a significant impact. However, the difference in the economic impacts between these three and construction is large. We feel confident in the distinction between construction-related activities and the other three categories.

Step 2: Estimate the Economic Impacts of Various Implementation Scenarios

The second step was to estimate the economic impacts of a set of scenarios based on potential implementation approaches for the recovery plan. We opted to apply an input–output model of Puerto Rico's economic conditions, using 2016 data provided by IMPLAN.[3] Input–output analysis is a standard technique that has been used for decades to estimate the regional economic impact of shocks to the supply chain. Given that input–output models are linear in design, these results can be scaled to reflect any level of spending.[4]

Although the time lag of the IMPLAN data set is not ideal because the baseline data are from before the hurricanes, the data in this model represent the best available estimates on sector-level production functions in Puerto Rico. We aggregated the industries in the input–output model to the two-digit NAICS code sectors to maintain consistency between our allocation of COAs, the macroeconomic impact estimation, and our eventual occupational analysis. We built our outcome scenarios to analyze five annual spending levels, in 2019 dollars: $1 billion, $2 billion, $5 billion, $10 billion, and $25 billion. This approach is appropriate because the recovery efforts are likely to have significant variance in yearly expenditures. Because up-front spending could be much greater than subsequent-year expenditures, we sought to understand how a nonconstant path of funding would affect labor demand in Puerto Rico.

Given that $1 billion of spending does not have a $1 billion effect on Puerto Rico's economy, we used input–output models to estimate the effects that spending injections or reductions have on an entire economy. In the case of an isolated market, such as Puerto Rico, it is important to consider the local purchasing ability of the economy because imports to Puerto Rico have a different effect on the economy from that of locally produced inputs. Demands not met by local production will "leak" out of the economy, reducing the economic impact on Puerto Rico. Significant proportions of spending go to paying workers for labor and buying material inputs from both local and nonlocal locations. By tracking these exchanges, we could estimate how much of the actual spending would leave the market and how much would be used to purchase goods from local industries. We assumed that the proportions of imported goods in each sector before and after the injection were the same. The local expansion is the indirect effect of the injection. In contrast, worker wages, proprietor profit, and other payments to capital increase the demand for all goods as a result of the increases in

---

[3] IMPLAN is an input–output modeling platform that downscales Bureau of Economic Analysis (BEA) national-level data to the local level. For further information about IMPLAN data and models, see IMPLAN, undated. Although more-recent data are available, they were not at the time of the analysis. Because we were conducting impact analysis, as long as the underlying sectoral production functions have not significantly changed, our results should be consistent with the more-recent 2018 data.

[4] Input–output models assume that all inputs to production are perfect complements and that consumption goods are perfect complements to household demand. Thus, to double output, we have to double every input. Although this assumption is convenient, it might not be valid in practice. However, it provides us with a first-order estimate of the likely impacts.

income, described above as the induced effect. The combined effects of direct, indirect, and induced increases to production represent the total economic impact of the initial injection.

We measured these economic impacts in four dimensions: output, value added, employee compensation, and employment:

- *Output* is the value of all goods and services that results from the increased spending, including all intermediate inputs. For example, if the economy produces $1 million worth of roads and uses $500,000 worth of locally produced concrete to build them, the total output for the economy would be $1.5 million. However, the exchange and product do not add $1.5 million worth of real value because we were counting the $500,000 worth of concrete twice in terms of concrete output and a portion of road output. As a result, we focused our attention on value added: the value of the good produced minus the cost of intermediate good and service inputs.
- *Value added* consists of such factors as proprietor income, employee compensation, payments to land, and taxes on production. This value estimate is similar to measures of gross domestic product (GDP) for countries or, for subcountry regions, gross regional product.
- Employee compensation was analyzed to gain a better understanding of how working people in Puerto Rico would fare from recovery spending.
- Changes in *employment* were obtained from both aggregate and sector data.

Step 3: Translate the Increased Employment to Increases in Occupational Demand

Our third step was to translate the increases in employment into increases in demand for specific occupations. Even though Puerto Rico had willing and able workers, they might not be in the specific occupations that would be needed for the recovery. To better understand these critical occupations, we used BLS's occupation-by-industry breakdowns (BLS, 2021 [2018 data]). These data are based on national-level data and are not Puerto Rico–specific, but they provide a suitable representation of occupations by industry. We provided these occupational demands using the two-digit and six-digit Standard Occupational Classification (SOC) system codes. With an understanding of these occupational needs, we compared the demands induced by the recovery spending with the current distribution of occupations in Puerto Rico.

Further leveraging BLS data, we calculated the wage disparity by occupation between Puerto Rico and the continental United States (CONUS), focusing on the six most common states of residence for immigrants from Puerto Rico.

Input–Output Model to Estimate Aggregate Demand from Recovery Spending

We first considered the output for a $1 billion (in 2019 dollars) annual recovery expenditure. Table 2.2 provides the aggregate results for this new spending. With the proportional allocation in the governor's 2018 recovery plan, this analysis suggests that a $1 billion expenditure would add approximately $1.2 billion to Puerto Rico's GDP and result in roughly 21,000 new jobs. However, note that, because the IMPLAN data are based on BEA data, these positions are not full-time equivalents but include counts of all full- and part-time jobs based on BEA industry average estimates.

Applying this same approach, we estimated the impacts for four additional expenditure levels: $2 billion, $5 billion, $10 billion, and $25 billion. Table 2.3 displays only the total effect for each of the expenditure scenarios. Given the linear nature of the input–output model, these are simply linear expansions of the initial case. Therefore, any of the results in Table 2.2 can be scaled easily to gain additional detail.

Table 2.4 displays the expected employment increases, by industry sector, for each of the recovery expenditures. Although it might seem odd that the administrative and waste management sector increase is more than double that of construction jobs, construction represents only 50 percent of the direct expenditures. Other sectors rely on the administrative and waste management sector as part of their inputs to production, including construction.

The June 2018 BLS estimate (BLS, undated a, series LASST720000000000006) reported the size of Puerto Rico's labor force as approximately 1.1 million workers. Given this number, considerable wage adjustments would need to be made in the larger-expenditure scenarios to incentivize unemployed residents of Puerto Rico or those working in the informal sector to take these jobs. For example, in the $10 billion–expenditure scenario, Puerto Rico would need to add approximately 46,000 construction workers in addition to the 27,000 construction workers currently employed there (BLS, undated a, series SMS72000001500000001). This is a significant increase, and Puerto Rico might not have the labor capacity to fill these

TABLE 2.2

Aggregate Economic Impact of a $1 Billion Recovery Expenditure in Puerto Rico

Effect Type	Employment	Effect, in Millions of 2019 Dollars		
		Labor Income	Value Added	Output
Direct	15,000	484	692	1,016
Indirect	2,000	66	170	250
Induced	4,000	135	329	483
Total	21,000	686	1,192	1,751

SOURCE: IMPLAN data.

NOTE: Totals do not equal the sum of the parts because of rounding.

TABLE 2.3

Total Effects of Alternative Recovery Expenditures

Expenditure, in Millions of 2019 Dollars	Employment	Effect, in Millions of 2019 Dollars		
		Labor Income	Value Added	Output
1,000	21,000	686	1,192	1,751
2,000	42,000	1,373	2,385	3,502
5,000	105,000	3,432	5,962	8,755
10,000	210,000	6,864	11,925	17,509
25,000	524,900	17,161	29,811	43,773

SOURCE: IMPLAN data.

jobs. In that case, incentive structures would need to be drastically changed to ensure the appropriate mix of workers required for the recovery efforts, mostly in terms of wages. In Chapter Three, we return to this topic.

One of the key challenges in estimating the economic and employment impacts of recovery efforts in Puerto Rico is that both the electric and water utilities are government entities. Accordingly, the input–output data from IMPLAN and BEA report these sectors' output as government production rather than as utility output. Thus, our models underestimated the impact of government activities that have private-sector analogues, such as utilities.

Translation of Employment Needs to Occupations

To explore these results further, we focused on the $10 billion–per–year recovery expenditure scenario and used the occupation-by-industry data to estimate the occupation-specific employment quantity demand increases. More than 1,000 occupational codes are available in the BLS occupation-by-industry database for the United States (BLS, 2021). As a starting point, we considered only the two-digit SOC codes to reduce the number for exposition purposes. Table 2.5 provides the projected total employment, by occupation, for the $10 billion recovery efforts. Not surprisingly, there is considerable increased demand for office and administrative support, construction, and construction-support occupations, based on the expenditure in administrative, business management, and construction positions, that the recovery expenditures directly affect. Additional occupations, such as production, sales, and protection-related occupations (i.e., security around job sites), are driven largely by the indirect and induced effects of the recovery efforts.

Table 2.6 presents the projected occupational demand for each six-digit SOC code for the 30 occupations in highest demand. The fourth column of Table 2.6 presents 2016 employment figures for Puerto Rico as reported in the BLS Occupational Employment Statistics. In many of these top 30 occupations, there are demand increases of between 5 and nearly 250 percent, suggesting that considerable expansion across occupations would need to occur to absorb the recovery efforts into the economy. The recovery plan effect is the additional labor demand above current levels.

TABLE 2.4

Employment, by Industry, for Recovery Expenditures

Industry, with NAICS Code	Expenditure, in Billions of 2019 Dollars				
	1	2	5	10	25
11 Agriculture, forestry, fishing, and hunting	200	300	800	1,500	5,000
21 Mining, quarrying, and oil and gas extraction	0	0	0	0	—
22 Utilities	0	0	0	0	—
23 Construction	4,600	9,100	22,800	45,700	115,000
31–33 Manufacturing	600	1,200	3,000	6,000	15,000
42 Wholesale trade	200	500	1,200	2,400	5,000
44–45 Retail trade	1,100	2,200	5,400	10,900	27,500
48–49 Transportation and warehousing	200	300	800	1,600	5,000
51 Information	100	100	400	700	2,500
52 Finance and insurance	100	100	400	700	2,500
53 Real estate and rental and leasing	100	300	700	1,400	2,500
54 Professional, scientific, and technical services	300	600	1,600	3,200	7,500
55 Management of companies and enterprises	500	1,100	2,700	5,400	12,500
56 Administrative and support and waste management and remediation services	10,800	21,500	53,800	107,600	270,000
61 Educational services	300	600	1,500	3,000	7,500
62 Health care and social assistance	800	1,600	4,100	8,200	20,000
71 Arts, entertainment, and recreation	0	100	200	500	—
72 Accommodation and food services	700	1,400	3,500	6,900	17,500
81 Other services (except public administration)	100	300	700	1,500	2,500
92 Public administration	300	600	1,500	2,900	7,500
Total	21,000	42,000	105,000	210,000	525,000

SOURCE: IMPLAN data.

NOTE: Totals do not equal the sum of the parts because of rounding.

TABLE 2.5

Employment, by Occupation, for a $10 Billion Recovery Effort

SOC Code	Title	Jobs	
		Direct	Total
0	Total	153,900	210,000
43	Office and administrative support occupations	27,100	34,900
47	Construction and extraction occupations	31,000	31,700
37	Building and grounds cleaning and maintenance occupations	21,600	23,800
53	Transportation and material moving occupations	14,000	18,200
41	Sales and related occupations	7,000	15,000
51	Production occupations	10,100	14,400
33	Protective service occupations	9,000	9,700
11	Management occupations	6,900	9,500
13	Business and financial operations occupations	6,800	8,700
49	Installation, maintenance, and repair occupations	6,800	8,700
35	Food preparation and serving-related occupations	1,100	7,500
29	Health care practitioners and technical occupations	1,800	5,100
15	Computer and mathematical occupations	3,100	4,400
25	Educational instruction and library occupations	1,700	3,000
31	Health care support occupations	1,100	2,700
39	Personal care and service occupations	1,100	2,500
17	Architecture and engineering occupations	1,600	2,400
45	Farming, fishing, and forestry occupations	200	1,400
27	Arts, design, entertainment, sports, and media occupations	700	1,300
21	Community and social service occupations	300	900
19	Life, physical, and social science occupations	400	700
23	Legal occupations	400	600

SOURCES: Occupational Employment and Wage Statistics data (BLS, undated b).

TABLE 2.6

The 30 Highest-Demand Employment Positions, by Occupation, for a $10 Billion Effort

SOC Code	Title	Plan Effect	Positions, 2016	Percentage Increase
37-2011	Janitors and cleaners, except maids and housekeeping cleaners	11,701	28,640	41
33-9032	Security guards	8,311	25,110	33
53-7062	Laborers and freight, stock, and material movers, hand	8,139	10,000	81
43-4051	Customer service representatives	7,059	14,240	50
37-3011	Landscaping and groundskeeping workers	6,694	6,420	104
47-2061	Construction laborers	6,063	6,680	91
43-9061	Office clerks, general	5,845	22,530	26
47-2031	Carpenters	4,205	2,080	202
43-6014	Secretaries and administrative assistants, except legal, medical, and executive	3,968	21,110	19
11-1021	General and operations managers	3,648	5,850	62
41-2031	Retail salespersons	3,404	38,690	9
47-2111	Electricians	3,418	1,420	241
47-1011	First-line supervisors of construction trades and extraction workers	2,997	2,910	103
43-3031	Bookkeeping, accounting, and auditing clerks	2,660	7,950	33
41-3099	Sales representatives, services, all other	2,629	2,860	92
41-2011	Cashiers	2,521	31,960	8
47-2152	Plumbers, pipefitters, and steamfitters	2,506	540	464
51-2092	Team assemblers	2,443	—	—
53-3032	Heavy and tractor-trailer truck drivers	2,354	8,130	29
37-2012	Maids and housekeeping cleaners	2,196	2,700	81
43-5081	Stock clerks and order fillers	2,190	17,730	12
53-7064	Packers and packagers, hand	2,168	3,560	61
43-1011	First-line supervisors of office and administrative support workers	1,954	15,840	12
35-3021	Combined food preparation and serving workers, including fast food	1,869	15,200	12
51-9198	Helpers—production workers	1,805	1,450	125

Table 2.6—Continued

SOC Code	Title	Plan Effect	Positions, 2016	Percentage Increase
29-1141	Registered nurses	1,746	19,090	9
47-2073	Operating engineers and other construction equipment operators	1,690	1,690	100
41-9041	Telemarketers	1,686	—	—
49-9021	Heating, air conditioning, and refrigeration mechanics and installers	1,606	1,630	99
49-9071	Maintenance and repair workers, general	1,555	6,850	23

SOURCE: BLS data.

NOTE: The plan effect is the additional labor demand above current levels. Numbers might not sum to total because of rounding.

Wage Disparity Between Puerto Rico and the Continental United States

Our next step leveraged the data on wages by occupation by area available from BLS to construct two measures of the wage disparity between Puerto Rico and CONUS:

- The first compared Puerto Rico and U.S. occupation-specific mean annual wages.
- The second examined the wages in the six states with the most people migrating from Puerto Rico: Florida, New York, Pennsylvania, Connecticut, Massachusetts, and New Jersey (Echenique and Melgar, 2018).

For each of these two measures, we constructed the ratio of the wage in Puerto Rico to that in the overall United States and to the average for the six states. For example, wages for security guards in Puerto Rico are 60 percent of the national average. The results for the occupations listed in Table 2.6 appear in Table 2.7.

TABLE 2.7

Wage Disparity Between Puerto Rico and the United States Generally and the Six States with the Most Migration from Puerto Rico

SOC Code	Title	Wage Disparity, Ratio	
		National Average	Six States
37-2011	Janitors and cleaners, except maids and housekeeping cleaners	0.73	0.64
33-9032	Security guards	0.60	0.59
53-7062	Laborers and freight, stock, and material movers, hand	0.77	0.74

Table 2.7—Continued

SOC Code	Title	Wage Disparity, Ratio	
		National Average	Six States
43-4051	Customer service representatives	0.65	0.59
37-3011	Landscaping and groundskeeping workers	0.69	0.64
47-2061	Construction laborers	0.50	0.41
43-9061	Office clerks, general	0.66	0.61
47-2031	Carpenters	0.42	0.35
43-6014	Secretaries and administrative assistants, except legal, medical, and executive	0.60	0.54
11-1021	General and operations managers	0.72	0.59
41-2031	Retail salespersons	0.69	0.68
47-2111	Electricians	0.51	0.45
43-3031	Bookkeeping, accounting, and auditing clerks	0.58	0.53
41-3099	Sales representatives, services, all other	0.55	0.47
41-2011	Cashiers	0.81	0.78
51-2092	Team assemblers	0.61	0.61
53-3032	Heavy and tractor-trailer truck drivers	0.44	0.42
37-2012	Maids and housekeeping cleaners	0.80	0.70
43-5081	Stock clerks and order fillers	0.72	0.71
53-7064	Packers and packagers, hand	0.71	0.67
43-1011	First-line supervisors of office and administrative support workers	0.64	0.58
35-3021	Combined food preparation and serving workers, including fast food	0.82	0.77
51-9198	Helpers—production workers	0.69	0.69
29-1141	Registered nurses	0.50	0.44
41-9041	Telemarketers	0.65	0.60
49-9071	Maintenance and repair workers, general	0.56	0.51
13-1071	Human resources specialists	0.57	0.51
43-3011	Bill and account collectors	0.62	0.56
51-9199	Production workers, all other	0.61	0.62
35-3031	Waiters and waitresses	0.74	0.66

SOURCE: BLS data.

NOTE: Wage disparity is the ratio of the wage in Puerto Rico to the wage in the United States or to the wage in the six states that receive the most Puerto Rico migration.

In most construction occupations, workers in Puerto Rico earn about half of what they would be paid by working in their trades in CONUS. This dynamic implies that, once a worker has received the appropriate training or education for the job, that worker can earn about twice as much money working in CONUS as in Puerto Rico. As a result, training local workers might not be enough to develop the workforce necessary to implement the recovery efforts, and additional incentives centered on wages might be required to retain and sustain a sufficient workforce for the duration of the recovery effort. However, it should be noted that the cost of living in Puerto Rico is roughly 70 percent of the U.S. average (MyLifeElsewhere, undated). Thus, a portion of the wage disparity is eroded in the lower cost of living, but the lower cost of living does not fully offset the reduction in wages. Additionally, a construction worker brought from CONUS would be paid nearly twice as much, as well as paid per diem and a wage premium for working in Puerto Rico. Although the Davis–Bacon Act (Pub. L. 71-798, 1931) would apply to all of these projects, the Davis–Bacon wage—normally, the prevailing local wage—for construction in Puerto Rico is the federal minimum wage.

Focus on the Construction Industry

Construction efforts make up approximately half of the expected recovery expenditures. Thus, we determined the projected occupational demand for each six-digit SOC and the wage disparity for the construction occupations themselves. Table 2.8 presents these results for the ten construction occupations expected to be most affected by the recovery plan. The first line represents total figures for construction-related jobs. Our findings raise concerns about Puerto Rico's ability to adjust to the spending stimulus from recovery-related investments. Our results indicate that the demand for construction-related occupations is likely to double with a $10 billion annual effort. In particular, there will be considerable demand for highly skilled construction occupations, such as electricians, plumbers and pipefitters, carpenters, and steel workers. These occupations require significant training that might not be available in the short run in Puerto Rico. A doubling or more in the need for skilled occupations will place considerable stress on the recovery efforts with respect to construction-related activities.

Implications

As described above, the demand for workers will significantly increase as the recovery efforts in Puerto Rico expand with additional appropriations and investments. As of June 2019, the unemployment rate had fallen in Puerto Rico from a high of 12 percent 2016 to 7.7 percent, with the size of the labor force remaining fairly constant between December 2017 and June 2019 at approximately 100,000 (BLS, undated a, series LASST720000000000003). This trend suggests that the current recovery efforts are having a positive economic effect: Workers

TABLE 2.8
Construction Employment for a $10 Billion Recovery Effort

Education	Training	SOC Code	Title	Plan Effect	Positions, 2017	Percentage Increase	Wage Disparity, in Dollars
No formal educational credential	Short-term on-the-job training	47-2061	Construction laborers	6,063	6,680	91	0.50
	Moderate-term on-the-job training	47-2141	Painters, construction, and maintenance	1,288	530	243	0.58
		47-2051	Cement masons and concrete finishers	1,163	620	188	0.42
		47-2181	Roofers	786	340	231	0.45
High school diploma or equivalent	None	47-1011	First-line supervisors of construction trades and extraction workers	2,997	2,910	103	0.43
	Moderate-term on-the-job training	47-2073	Operating engineers and other construction equipment operators	1,690	1,690	100	0.45
	Apprenticeship	47-2031	Carpenters	4,205	2,080	202	0.42
		47-2111	Electricians	3,418	1,420	241	0.51
		47-2152	Plumbers, pipefitters, and steamfitters	2,506	540	464	0.39
		47-2211	Sheet metal workers	669	130	515	0.50
		47-0000	All construction	31,700	27,410	116	0.44

SOURCE: BLS data.

NOTE: The plan effect is the additional labor demand above current levels. For hazardous material–removal workers, no data for Puerto Rico are available (they are suppressed for proprietary reasons).

looking for employment are now more likely to find it. We expect that, as the recovery efforts increase, this movement will continue.

Approximately 100,000 people in Puerto Rico were unemployed as of June 2019 (BLS, undated a, series LASST720000000000004). If Puerto Rico were to achieve the CONUS unemployment level of approximately 4 percent, another 60,000 workers would be available without a commensurate increase in labor supply. However, our research indicates that the skill mismatch between labor demand and labor supply within the distribution of occupations will likely present challenges for recovery demands. Nevertheless, given that most of the occupations in demand have minimal educational and training requirements, these currently unemployed workers will likely find work. For jobs with more-intensive educational or training requirements, programs should be developed to train the needed workers. The programs could be driven by policy or through market demand, as long as sufficient expertise is available. At present, there is no incentive to fill labor demands with local labor: According to a 2018 report from the Center for a New Economy, more than 90 percent of recovery contract dollars went to CONUS firms (Lamba-Nieves and Santiago-Bartolomei, 2018). The need for construction trades to satisfy the requirements of the current recovery plan is significant, and these occupations will require considerable training.

Although there will be considerable demand for all skills, workers who receive either formal or on-the-job training will have an incentive (greater wages) to move to CONUS once these skills are acquired. According to anecdotal evidence, this already occurs with nurses and bilingual hospitality workers (Milligan, 2018). If formal training is to be provided for recovery support positions, incentives will be needed to keep trained workers in Puerto Rico.

We expect that, as recovery efforts expand and the unemployment rate continues to decline, subsequent wage pressures will increase wages to meet the increased demand. This effect should encourage some of the people currently not in the labor force to participate, expanding the labor supply and slowing the rate of increase of wages. At present, the prime working-age (i.e., 25–34 and 35–44) labor force participation rates are 73 percent and 72 percent, respectively. In comparison to CONUS at 82, they are considerably lower (Gonzalez et al., 2020). If the scale of the recovery efforts is sufficiently large, labor demand pressures could increase wages across Puerto Rico sufficiently to erase historical wage disparities. This achievement would result in the return of previous emigrants to Puerto Rico and could encourage others in CONUS to seek opportunities in Puerto Rico.

According to Table 2.8, the construction labor force would need to increase by 116 percent from the baseline. Additionally, for the more-skilled occupations, such as electricians and plumbers, the labor demands are 200 to 500 percent above baseline employment. The skilled labor makes up approximately half of the increase in demand. Unless training programs can be established for these skilled occupations, workers will need to come from outside of Puerto Rico. Thus, it is possible that, based on both the occupational mix and scale of the efforts, approximately 75 percent of the labor force needed for the recovery efforts will likely come from CONUS. As a result, we should take this into account to estimate construction costs correctly.

CHAPTER THREE

Estimating Expenditure Scenarios

As part of estimating the effects that recovery efforts are likely to have on the economy, the scale and timing of investments are important to know. If the size of the reconstruction efforts is small compared with that of the construction sector, there might be no impact. On the other hand, if reconstruction operations are ramped up quickly, significant price increases might need to be considered when developing fixed-price estimates. Because no schedule was developed with the plan, we used historical data on hurricane obligations from FEMA's PA program to build an expenditure simulator to serve as an input to an economywide model. This allowed us to develop a set of potential expenditure paths that were consistent with previous FEMA efforts while building in potential capacity constraints that are described more fully in how we incorporate different scenarios for María expenditures.

Estimating Yearly Expenditures

To estimate the amount of spending on the recovery in each year, we used data from the Emergency Management Mission Integrated Environment (EMMIE) system.[1] EMMIE is a web-based tool that allows grantees to submit documentation necessary for compensation for completed PA work. The system allows PA recipients to "complete, submit, monitor, and manage Public Assistance applications online" (FEMA, 2021a) and has records of PA expenditures from previous natural disasters. We focused on projects larger than $1 million and excluded from the analysis disasters for which there was evidence of ongoing work on PA.[2] The reason for the focus on projects larger than $1 million was that we were more confident in the dates of project execution and completion than we were for smaller projects. Large

---

[1] Note that, although EMMIE was fully implemented in 2008, the previous system data from the National Emergency Management Information System were migrated to EMMIE. This might have resulted in some data loss or incompatibility; however, we did not find any evidence that the data from before 2008 were of poorer quality than the more-recent data.

[2] More precisely, we excluded disasters for which work on PA was dated to have been completed in the previous three years (2017 through 2019). We viewed this as an indication that the disaster had other projects that remained to be done, whereas disasters for which work was completed earlier than the previous three years—and for which no work had been completed within the previous three years—were assumed to be complete. We used this method because "in-progress" projects in the EMMIE data are not labeled as such.

projects constitute the majority of PA spending (e.g., they accounted for roughly 75 percent of the total expenditures for Hurricane Sandy), and they correlate strongly with the overall PA spending (e.g., variation in the amount of expenditures on large projects can explain roughly 80 percent of the variation in total expenditures).

We conducted an analysis of the historical spending paths for all hurricanes since 2000. To understand typical spending paths, we aggregated the individual PA projects into a measure of yearly expenditures for each hurricane. We calculated spending paths by hurricane, even if there were multiple disaster declarations for the same hurricane. This allowed us to calculate the value of expenditures occurring in the first 365 days after a disaster declaration separately from the value of expenditures occurring in the second 365 days and subsequent years.

To make these calculations, we needed to date each project, which was challenging given that the EMMIE data on which we relied did not clearly identify the date of work completion for the project and instead identified relevant administrative dates, such as the date the money was obligated and the date the project was officially closed. The data we used contain information on the percentage of the project completed as of a particular date, which was nearly always listed as 0 percent or 100 percent. For the roughly 60 percent of projects for which the percentage complete was listed as 100 percent, we used the specified date as a latest bound on the date when the work was conducted. Placing a date on the other 40 percent of projects was more challenging. For these projects, we used a variable that measures when the funds were allocated to the applicant.[3]

We calculated the spending path of each previous hurricane by dividing the expenditure amount in a given year by the total expenditures.[4] Figure 3.1 illustrates the cumulative spending paths, which show the fraction of spending up to and including the given year for all the hurricanes used in the analysis and explicitly highlights Hurricanes Katrina and Sandy. In addition to the aggregate spending paths shown in the figure, we estimated the spending paths separately for four categories of PA: roads and bridges (category C), water (category D), buildings (category E),[5] and utilities (category F).

It is worth noting explicitly that the difficulties in dating the expenditures mean that any estimated spending path should be viewed as a noisy *estimate* of the true spending path, rather than the true spending path itself. Although we plan to conduct further work to better estimate the individual spending paths of previous disasters, for our purposes here, we needed to accurately represent only the range of possible expenditure paths in Puerto Rico. Thus, as

---

[3] More specifically, we used a field in the EMMIE data called "Award Date," which seems to align with the date the project was awarded and the money was allocated.

[4] Note that this assumed that the total amount of expenditures in the EMMIE data was equal to the total expenditures, which would be invalid if spending were still occurring. This is why we omitted recent disasters that still appeared to be spending on PA. If additional expenditures were made, the curves illustrated in Figure 3.1, as used in our analysis, would be lower bounds on the true expenditure curves.

[5] Category G (parks and recreational facilities) was added to category E.

FIGURE 3.1

Obligation Curves for Hurricanes Katrina, Sandy, and All Other Hurricanes

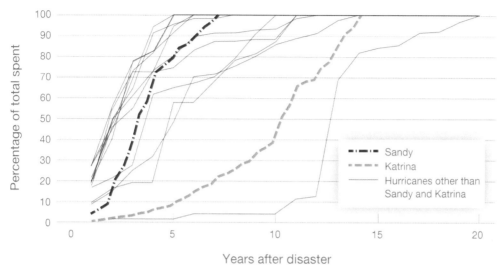

SOURCE: EMMIE data.

NOTE: Because of limitations of the EMMIE data, the figure shows the range of feasible expenditure paths, not an accurate estimate of any particular spending path.

long as our approach did not consistently over- or underestimate the expenditure paths, we still generated a valid FPF. Because approximately 60 percent of our estimates overestimated the time to completion and 40 percent likely underestimated it, we anticipate that these errors will be somewhat offsetting and will result in minimal systematic bias.[6]

Given these estimated expenditure paths, to introduce a stochastic component, we then randomly sampled a series of feasible spending paths from the discrete number of spending paths. To do so, we employed the use of hazard rates, which we calculated as the percentage of remaining expenditures that were spent in the specified period. For example, if 25 percent of the overall expenditures were made in the first four years and an additional 10 percent of the expenditures were made in the fifth year, the hazard rate in the fifth year would be calculated as

$$N\left(\hat{\beta}, \sigma_{\hat{\beta}}^2\right)$$

---

[6] Separate analysis of Hurricane Sandy spending supports our analysis of the EMMIE data. We found that both the total dollar amount and spending rates were captured reasonably well in our EMMIE data analysis. Our analysis of spending plans using New Jersey data showed that early spending was completed more slowly than in EMMIE data but that later spending accelerated and was completed more quickly. Overall, the bulk of the spending occurred approximately eight months earlier in the New Jersey data than in the EMMIE data. We can think of these obligation paths as functioning as lead expenditure paths. Thus, by assuming that year 0 was 2019, we took into account the administrative and design time in moving from obligation to expenditures.

which equals 0.133. Denoting the hazard rate in year t for disaster i for category c as h_{itc}, we then modeled the overall hazard rate as a combination of disaster, year, and category fixed effects. Note that, here, *year* refers to the number of years after the disaster, rather than the calendar year. This can be written as

$$h_{itc} = \alpha_i + \beta_t + \gamma_c + \epsilon_{itc}. \tag{3.1}$$

This parameterization of the hazard rate means that we reduced the dimensionality of the speed of expenditures for each disaster into one parameter: α_i. β_t is time fixed effects, and γ_c is storm fixed effects. ϵ_{itc} is stochastic error terms.

Our final step in the spending path simulation was to use the estimates of the disaster, year, and category fixed effects, as well as the uncertainty surrounding their estimates, to simulate several hypothetical spending distributions. We randomly chose a hurricane from the list of previous hurricanes. We then determined the disaster-level fixed effect for this simulation by taking a random draw from the normal distribution centered as the estimated fixed effect for the (randomly) determined hurricane and a standard deviation equal to the standard error of the fixed-effect estimate. Given this disaster-level fixed effect, we then randomly drew time fixed effects and category fixed effects from the distributions $N\left(\hat{\beta}, \sigma_{\hat{\beta}}^2\right)$ and $N\left(\hat{\gamma}, \sigma_{\hat{\gamma}}^2\right)$, where $\hat{\beta}$ is the vector of estimated time fixed effects and $\sigma_{\hat{\beta}}^2$ is the estimated variance–covariance matrix of these estimates; $\hat{\gamma}$ and $\sigma_{\hat{\gamma}}^2$ are defined similarly.

These draws gave a random combination of the disaster, year, and category fixed effects, which allowed us to generate hazard rates using Equation 3.1. From these hazard rates, we could then generate a full spending path, using the hazard rates to calculate the unconditional fraction of expenditures in each period and then multiplying that by the overall expenditure amount of $50 billion. We note that there was also considerable uncertainty around the anticipated $50 billion in permanent-work PA expenditures expected for Puerto Rico.[7]

Adjustments to the Spending Path to Better Mimic Hurricane María

This spending path can be thought of as a random sample from the set of feasible spending paths informed by the spending paths of the previous hurricanes. To reflect the unique characteristics of Hurricane María, we made two additional adjustments.

First, given the limited amount of PA expenditures in the first few years following Hurricane María, we included only spending paths for which less than 25 percent of the overall spending was completed in the first two years.

---

[7] This was calculated based on the roughly $50 billion in construction estimated from the governor's 2018 recovery plan discussed in Chapter Two.

Second, we included capacity constraints in the spending path estimation to ensure that we were not predicting an unreasonable amount of spending in Puerto Rico in a particular year (we relaxed this assumption later). Our expenditure constraints were as follows:

- $2 billion in the first year
- $4 billion in the second year
- $6 billion in the third year
- $8 billion in the fourth year
- 5-percent growth in capacity in the subsequent years.

If the simulated spending path predicted an expenditure in excess of capacity, the excess capacity was added to the subsequent year. For example, if the simulated spending path predicted expenditures of $7 billion in year 3, we assumed that only $6 billion would be spent in year 3 and the excess of $1 billion would instead be spent in year 4, along with the additional money that the spending path predicted to be spent in year 4.

In addition to this specification, to which we refer as the *baseline* or *constrained* spending path in the results in Figure 3.2, we ran three additional specifications:

- In the first, which we call the *unconstrained* specification, we removed the capacity constraints described above.
- In the second, which we call *aggressive*, we both removed the capacity constraints and included spending paths on which less than 50 percent (rather than 25 percent) of the overall spending was completed in the first two years.
- In the third and final, which we call the *superaggressive*, we both removed the capacity constraints and included all spending paths, regardless of how much was spent in the first two years.

Using the described approach, we constructed 100 simulations of potential spending distributions for each of the four PA categories described above: roads and bridges (category C), water (category D), buildings (category E), and utilities (category F). Figure 3.2 provides an average of the aggregate distribution of expenditures across the four categories of expenditure plans described above to highlight how alternative assumptions manifest in the expenditure curves. We then used these spending paths as inputs to the model described in Chapter Four.

One final note is that, when we applied these spending paths to the model, we assumed that year 0 of the simulated spending path corresponded to 2019, even though Hurricane María occurred in 2017. This was to reconcile the fact that little PA spending had occurred in Puerto Rico with the fact that a relatively large fraction of PA expenditures occurs in the first two years after other disasters. If the two-year period of minimal expenditures used in the baseline scenario is indicative of a longer ramp-up period in the subsequent years as well, our simulations would produce expenditure plans that are too aggressive.

FIGURE 3.2

Average Expenditure for Each Assumption, in Billions of Dollars

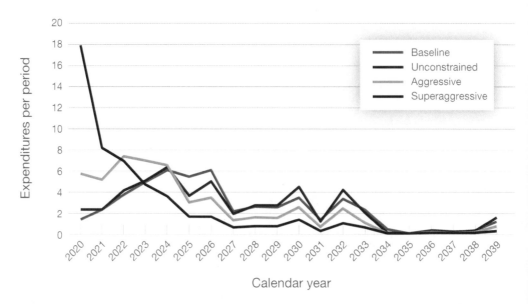

CHAPTER FOUR

The Computable General Equilibrium Model

Our approach to the development of a CGE model is based on Nadreau, 2015; Rausch and Rutherford, 2008; and Sue Wing, 2007. We used the IMPLAN Social Accounting Matrix (SAM) for Puerto Rico to calibrate the initial values of parameters within the model. We used data for 2016 because they were the most recently available at the time of this analysis; the next–most recent data were from 2010.[1] IMPLAN data are based on the national-level input–output tables developed by BEA and then downscaled to the local levels based on a proprietary algorithm. IMPLAN has been a staple of regional economics for the past 30 years.[2]

The IMPLAN data provide calibration values for 536 sectors. To deliver a manageable modeling process and ensure a clear interpretation of results, we aggregated the 536 sectors to five construction sectors and nine nonconstruction sectors, as recommended in the methodology implemented by Nadreau, 2015, with the five construction sectors roughly corresponding to the PA permanent-work categories. Each sector is viewed as having a representative firm that is assumed to maximize profit, implying that it uses the least-cost combination of inputs needed to produce its output. It is further assumed that the firm is a price-taker in a competitive market and that the sector is in equilibrium (e.g., the amount supplied equals the amount demanded). The IMPLAN data not only provide consumption and earnings for a single representative household but also offer relevant data for both state and federal governments. Households are assumed to maximize utility, taking good and factor prices as given. Finally, markets clear as prices adjust, with global prices assumed constant for imports and exports. Thus, we assumed that Puerto Rico was a small, open economy that did not affect

---

[1] At present, no good estimates exist for GDP in 2018 for Puerto Rico. The Economic Development Bank of Puerto publishes an economic activity index (EAI) that is a coincident index of GDP. During 2010, the average EAI was 135; in 2016, it was 124; and, in 2018, it was 120. Thus, we believe that, given the significant economic decline that has occurred in Puerto Rico since 2006, it seems more appropriate to use the 2016 data than the 2010 data to model 2018 and beyond. If there is significant economic development in the coming years, it might make sense to use the 2010 data or those from a more recent year, if data are available.

[2] Recently, Thomas Rutherford and Andrew Schreiber have developed an open-source method for downscaling the BEA tables, but we have not sufficiently vetted this algorithm to determine whether it provides advantages over the IMPLAN data. Further information on this approach is available at Rutherford and Schreiber, undated. Additionally, Puerto Rico provides an interesting case in that BEA does not directly collect data in Puerto Rico, and we have found no data sources besides IMPLAN that provide SAMs for Puerto Rico.

global prices, despite the considerable expansions required for Puerto Rico's economy in its recovery efforts. Our approach was to build a static general equilibrium model of the economy of Puerto Rico and introduce transition dynamics through adjustments to the labor and capital stocks, *across periods.*

Model Specification

The Producer's Problem

In developing our calculation, we modeled the production in each sector, *i*, as a representative firm that had chosen its output to maximize profit at a given price. In our model, firms are assumed to be perfectly competitive.[3] The production process follows a nested, constant-elasticity-of-substitution (CES) function, as depicted in Figure 4.1.[4] At the bottom level, construction and nonconstruction labor were combined using the estimates in Chapter Five to form a labor composite. This labor composite was then combined with capital using Cobb–Douglas technology to create a techno-labor composite because the literature suggests that capital and labor are different from materials in the production process, following Nadreau. A Cobb–Douglas production function has certain properties that make it a good choice for use in this type of analysis: It is convex and monotonic and provides computationally tractable estimates of technical rates of substitution (Varian, 1992).[5] Next, intermediate goods were combined in another nest and then combined with the techno-labor composite using Leontief technology, following Nadreau. The Leontief technology assumes that intermediate goods are complements in production. Typically, intermediate goods are thought of inputs to the production process and are used on a one-to-one basis with the labor–capital input.

Overall, this structure allows wages to vary across sectors and by experience type. The composite labor function allows relative wages to depend on the amounts of construction and nonconstruction labor available in the economy and accounts for their relative productivity. Moreover, relative wages *adjust* as the amounts and productivity of each labor type change over time. The benchmark factor shares of construction and nonconstruction labor are estimated from the CPS, which is used to estimate the changes in employment by industry from month-to-month changes in industry at the individual level. We collapsed industries

---

[3] We made this assumption for a variety of reasons. First, it is probably true to a first approximation: There are many small firms, there is a lack of unionization, and market entry and exit are fairly easy. However, there are other actors that have some market power. The supply chains have fewer providers: ships, ports, warehouses, and transport. In particular, concrete has few suppliers and is a significant user of energy, which has significantly fewer providers. However, modeling market power is highly complex; we assumed perfect competition as a good first approximation and for computational tractability.

[4] From 2018 to 2020, there were approximately 2,100 private construction establishments in Puerto Rico (BLS, 2019, series ENU720002051012).

[5] Let a be a parameter such that $0 < a < 1$ then the Cobb–Douglas technology is defined as $q = L^a K^{1-a}$ where q is the output quantity and L and K are labor and capital inputs, respectively.

FIGURE 4.1
Production Functions in Each Sector

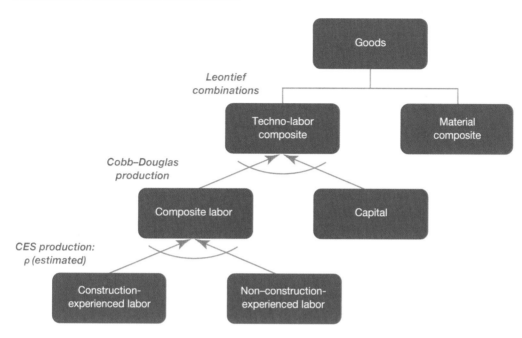

into construction and nonconstruction sectors. These estimates suggest that approximately 0.2 percent of the labor force switches from construction to nonconstruction and vice versa. Thus, we allocated the baseline industry labor for each of the construction and nonconstruction sectors to match this. This implies that approximately 10 percent of the workers in construction were not in construction the previous year, based on the relative sizes of the construction and nonconstruction labor forces.

The Consumer's Problem

The consumer's problem is quite similar to the producer's problem. We assumed that a representative household maximizes utility, receiving income from the factors of production (capital and labor), net sales of exports, transfer payments from either federal or state governments, and investments in inventory. We assumed that the utility function was simply a Cobb–Douglas utility function, calibrated to the consumption data in the IMPLAN data following Nadreau, 2015; Rausch and Rutherford, 2008; and Sue Wing, 2007. Like with the production function, for which labor and capital are inputs, we assumed that individuals convert consumption of good and services (D) into utility. Because individuals consume many of these types of items, the Cobb–Douglas production function can be converted by means of logarithm, and the α are assumed to sum to less than 1. We normalized the amount of labor and capital to the 2016 levels:

$$U_{it} = \Sigma_i \alpha_i \ln(D_{it}), \tag{4.1}$$

where α_i is the budget share of good i in the benchmark data and D_{it} is household demand for good i in time period t.

Puerto Rico's Problem

Puerto Rico was assumed to receive tax revenue and to provide goods and transfer payments that were consistent and unchanged during the recovery efforts. However, this is not necessarily true because construction efforts provide considerable revenue through additional income taxes and through construction taxes. To consider the effects of recovery spending, we modified the Puerto Rico problem slightly to meet the needs of the following scenarios. Under this dynamic, Puerto Rico both spends funds and receives payments from the federal government, as is consistent with our analysis scenarios. This process increases demand without placing a fiscal burden on Puerto Rico. That is, if Puerto Rico is to produce $5 billion worth of construction (in 2019 dollars), it receives $5 billion times the price of construction. For example, if construction prices rose 20 percent, Puerto Rico would receive a transfer of $6 billion from the federal government and fulfill $5 billion worth of construction demand. Thus, if no FPF were applied, the project would be underfunded by $1 billion, which would be Puerto Rico's responsibility. Our approach attempted to reconcile this disparity by considering the suite of projects rather than any one project.

Equilibrium

We calibrated the model to the initial conditions defined by the SAM produced from the IMPLAN data. The SAM included not only the baseline production inputs but also the consumption inputs and links between ownership of factors of production, such as capital and labor. The static model was written in the General Algebraic Modeling System using the Mathematical Programming System for General Equilibrium subsystem and uses the PATH solver. An equilibrium is characterized by a set of good and factor prices together with market-clearing levels of production and consumption. In equilibrium, there might be imported factors: The aggregate demand shocks to the system from the recovery efforts might be too large for the factor endowments to absorb. Given the small, open-economy assumption, this did not pose a problem.

Construction Subsectors

With the available IMPLAN production data for Puerto Rico, we next separated construction into the following subsectors, each of which maps to a related spending category for PA:

- category C (roads and bridges)
- category D (water control facilities)
- categories E (buildings and equipment) and G (parks and recreation facilities)

- category F (utilities)
- other (residential construction).

This structure allowed us to examine the impacts of recovery spending plans as they vary across PA categories.

Collapsing All Other Sectors

In keeping with Nadreau, 2015, the nonconstruction sectors were aggregated into nine sectors:

- agriculture
- utilities
- fossil fuels
- wholesale and retail trade
- mining and quarrying
- processed food
- manufacturing
- services
- miscellaneous.

CHAPTER FIVE

Estimating Construction and Nonconstruction Labor Substitutability

Given the labor supply constraints discussed in Chapter Two, wages will likely need to increase in the construction sector. And if wages rise within the construction sector, some labor is likely to move from nonconstruction jobs into construction jobs. From a production standpoint, inexperienced workers might be less productive than experienced construction workers. Given our goal of building a CGE model of Puerto Rico's economy to estimate price impacts, we needed to find a way to represent the imperfect substitutability of experienced and nonexperienced labor in a CGE model.

The aim of this chapter is to describe our use of econometric methods to estimate a substitution elasticity between construction and nonconstruction labor, which we defined as ρ. This would then be used as an input within the CGE model, as in Figure 4.1 in Chapter Four. This chapter is important because this elasticity was unknown yet crucial for the CGE model. No previous research has done this, and we were therefore required to correctly calibrate this parameter, rather than simply "inventing" a number.

To do so, we endowed households with labor differentiated by sectoral experience and set the economy to produce an intermediate, composite labor good for each sector. This composite labor good was produced according to a CES production function, taking non–construction-experienced and construction-experienced labor as inputs. Succinctly,

$$L_t^S = \left(\theta_c l_{c,t}^\rho + \theta_{nc} l_{nc,t}^\rho \right)^{\frac{1}{\rho}},$$ (5.1)

where L_t^S is the composite labor supplied to sector S at time t; $l_{c,t}$ denotes construction-experienced labor; $l_{nc,t}$ denotes non–construction-experienced labor; θ_c and θ_{nc} are the respective productive shares of the experience types, such that $\theta_c + \theta_{nc} = 1$; and ρ is related to an elasticity-of-substitution parameter that measures the substitutability of construction-experienced labor for non–construction-experienced labor within the economy. When ρ approaches 0, the CES function converges to a Cobb–Douglas production function, and, when ρ approaches negative infinity, the CES function degenerates to a Leontief function.

Overall, this structure allows wages to vary across sectors and by experience type. The composite labor function allows relative wages to depend on the amounts of construction and nonconstruction labor available in the economy and accounts for the differences in their relative productivity. Moreover, relative wages adjust as the amounts and productivity of each labor type change over time.

As we described in Chapter Four, the ρ parameter is related to the elasticity of substitution and was estimated in accordance with Katz and Murphy, 1992, using the March CPS data from 1980 to 2018 (U.S. Census Bureau, undated). The benchmark factor shares are estimated from the CPS for the entire United States, which is used to estimate the changes in employment by industry from year-to-year changes in industry at the individual level. We collapsed industries into construction and nonconstruction sectors. These estimates suggest that approximately 0.2 percent of the labor force switches from construction to nonconstruction and vice versa. Thus, we allocated the baseline industry labor for each of the construction and nonconstruction sectors to match this. This implies that approximately 10 percent of the workers in construction were not in construction the previous period.

To implement the composite labor given in Equation 5.1, the ρ parameter must be estimated separately. We describe here how we roughly followed Katz and Murphy, 1992, to estimate the elasticity of substitution between different types of labor. Note that the elasticity of substitution, σ, for the composite labor production function in Equation 5.1 is given by

$$\sigma = \frac{1}{1-\rho}.$$

Taking derivatives of the composite labor production function with respect to each labor type and setting those marginal products equal to wages (which assumes perfect competition) results in the following relationship, which must hold in equilibrium in each time period t:

$$\ln\left(\frac{w_{ct}}{w_{nct}}\right) = \ln\left(\frac{\theta_{ct}}{\theta_{nct}}\right) - \frac{1}{\sigma}\ln\left(\frac{l_{ct}}{l_{nct}}\right).$$

The elasticity of substitution is assumed to be constant over time and is thus identified by relative changes in labor supply and wages of construction-experienced workers versus non–construction-experienced workers over time. This relationship represents conditional factor demands, in which other factors besides labor have been excluded. The demand shifters,

$$\frac{\theta_{ct}}{\theta_{nct}},$$

thus incorporate any relative changes in the productivity of construction-experienced labor and non–construction-experienced labor, as well as any relative demand shifts for construction-experienced labor and non–construction-experienced labor. Following the literature on skilled versus nonskilled labor (Card and Lemieux, 2001; Katz and Murphy, 1992; K. Murphy and Welch, 1992), these shifters are specified as

$$\ln\left(\frac{w_{ct}}{w_{nct}}\right) = D(t) - \frac{1}{\sigma}\ln\left(\frac{l_{ct}}{l_{nct}}\right)$$

$$\ln\left(\frac{w_{ct}}{w_{nct}}\right) = \alpha_0 + \alpha_1 t + \gamma UNRES_t - \frac{1}{\sigma}\ln\left(\frac{l_{ct}}{l_{nct}}\right) + e_t.$$

This final equation serves as the estimating equation, where e_t reflects sampling variation in the relative wages or any other idiosyncratic variation in observed relative wages. This specification for the shifters can be understood as assuming that the relative efficiency is modeled to be linear in time and an unemployment residual, with an intercept α_0. Shocks to the unemployment rate over time could differentially affect the demand for construction-experienced labor and non–construction-experienced labor. This notion is captured in the $UNRES_t$ variable, which is the residual from an autoregressive (AR) model, AR(1), of the unemployment rate on its lag (K. Murphy and Welch, 1992).

The estimating equation was implemented using wage and labor supply data from the March CPS from 1980 through 2018 (U.S. Census Bureau, undated). Wages were measured as the average weekly wages for full-time workers ages 16 and older who were not self-employed. Labor supply was measured as the annual hours supplied by all workers, including part-time and self-employed. Annual hours were calculated by multiplying the number of usual hours worked per week by the number of weeks worked in the past year.

To account for productivity differences within labor type, a binning strategy was used (Card and Lemieux, 2001; Katz and Murphy, 1992). The data are divided into 30 distinct labor groups distinguished by gender and potential experience. Gender is a binary variable in this data set. Potential experience was divided into 15 bins based on five-year intervals starting with [0,4] years inclusive.[1] The ratio of relative wages of construction-experienced workers to those of non–construction-experienced workers was calculated from the March CPS data for each bin in each year. Aggregate relative wages in each year were then calculated by summing over the 30 weighted bins, where each bin was weighted by that bin's average share of employment over the entire period.

---

[1] Potential experience was calculated as $\max\left(\min\left(age-17, age - yearsofeducation - 7\right), 0\right)$, where *age* is the age at the date of the survey; this is consistent with Katz and Murphy, 1992. Before 1992, the March CPS coded education into five categories: less than high school, high school, some college, college degree, and advanced. For calculating potential experience, less than high school is assigned ten years of education, high school is assigned 12, some college is assigned 14, college degree is assigned 16, and advanced is assigned 18.

Similarly, relative labor supply was calculated within each bin for each year. Aggregate relative labor supply for each year was then calculated by summing over the bins, where each bin was weighted by the average relative wages earned by that bin over the entire period.

Efficiency units, rather than relative wage levels or relative hours, were used to account for productivity differences across gender–potential experience levels. Female workers with five years of potential experience might have different productivity from male workers with 15 years of potential experience. If only levels were used, each hour of labor supplied by women with five years of experience would be weighted the same as each hour supplied by men with 15 years of potential experience. Weighting the "female, [5,9] years" relative labor supply bin by that bin's average share of weekly wages over the period attempts to compare units with similar productivity (as measured by wages[2]), as opposed to comparing workers who might have different productivity levels. Similarly, weighting the "female, [5,9] years" relative wage bin by that bin's average share in total employment over the period before aggregating was an attempt to use efficiency units that are comparable across bins.

The binning and aggregating strategy described above yields a measure of relative wages per year and relative labor supply per year for each of the 38 years from 1980 through 2018. These variables were then used to estimate the estimating equation derived above, which followed from the composite labor structure in the CGE model. To implement the composite labor structure, an estimate of ρ was needed. The results from the estimating equation using the data described above are presented in Table 5.1. The coefficient of –0.124 on the relative labor supply corresponds to an elasticity of substitution of 8.05. (In comparison, perfect substitutes have an elasticity of substitution of infinity, and labor and capital in a classic Cobb–Douglas production function have an elasticity of substitution of 1.) Construction-experienced labor and non–construction-experienced labor were thus estimated to be imperfect substitutes. In terms of the updates to the model, the estimate of –0.124 corresponds to an estimate for ρ of 0.876, which is used in Equation 5.1. The coefficient for the elasticity is statistically significant, while that of year and *UNRES* are not.

---

[2] Recall that perfect competition was assumed; therefore, wages measure marginal factor productivity. The intent here is not to explain why different gender–potential experience bins might be differentially productive (in terms of wages) but instead to adjust for those differences in a way that estimates most accurately the elasticity of substitution between construction and nonconstruction labor.

TABLE 5.1

Estimation Results

Variable	Coefficient	Standard Error
Relative labor supply	−0.124	0.061
Year	0.000	0.001
UNRES	−0.005	0.006
Intercept	0.067	1.663

NOTE: $N = 38$. $R^2 = 0.244$. $F(3,34) = 3.655$. *Year* refers to calendar year, and relative labor supply is the ratio of aggregate construction labor supply, by year, to aggregate nonconstruction labor supply, by year, where the aggregation method is in terms of efficiency units, as explained in the text.

CHAPTER SIX

Results of the Modeling Approach

Using the expenditure simulations for the four assumption scenarios (baseline, unconstrained, aggressive, and superaggressive, as described in Chapter Three) together with the economywide model, we estimated the future prices of construction labor (wages), materials, and equipment. For each simulation (100 for each of our four assumptions), we ran the economywide model and captured results for wages, material prices, and equipment prices. We then created representative price paths for each scenario and component by smoothing our results: For each result set, we regressed an eighth-order polynomial expansion across time, with no constant, against model output minus 1.[1] A representative price path for a given scenario and component was then the predicted value from this regression plus 1.

Labor

Because there are five construction labor sectors in the model, each of which has the potential to use a different mix of construction and nonconstruction labor, and all PA expenditures will occur in only four of them, we took a simple average over wages for the composite labor in the four sectors employed in PA.[2] This gave us the average wages that expenditures for PA are likely to entail. Figure 6.1 summarizes the results for each of the four sets of simulations. Importantly, these are wages for the local labor force. As we discuss in Chapter Seven (on implementation), wages used in the estimation of construction costs will be a weighted average of local and modified CONUS-based wages because there is not likely to be the appropriate mix of skills necessary to carry out the projects using PA expenditures or the local labor supply for more-aggressive expenditure plans. As plans become more aggressive in the timing of expenditures, more CONUS-based labor will be needed to overcome more than just the lack of appropriate skills in the local labor force.

---

[1] This procedure allowed us to use all the output from the expenditure curves through the economywide model rather than simply using a single measure, such as the median expenditure. The polynomial approach gives us a smooth expenditure output and prevents large year-over-year swings. We used an eighth-order polynomial based on starting with a tenth order and eliminating higher-order terms until the highest-order term was significant at the 95th percentile.

[2] Although it would be preferable to take a weighted average, the differences across sectors are small enough that we used an arithmetic mean.

FIGURE 6.1

Estimated Local Average Wages for Public Assistance Projects

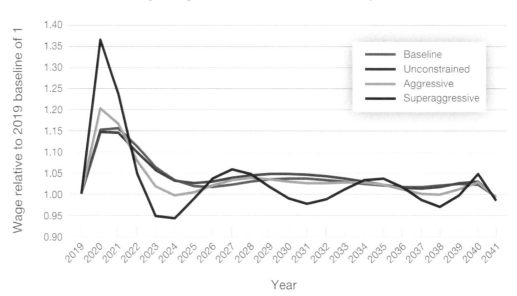

NOTE: The figure shows average wages for construction sets likely to be affected by PA expenditures, using the four sets of expenditure simulations. All wages are relative to a baseline wage of 1 in 2019.

The findings suggest the following observations:

- First, whether we assume a baseline, unconstrained, or aggressive expenditure plan, wages are not likely to be considerably different, although there is a clear increase in wages in the earliest years, depending on the aggressiveness of the expenditure plan.
- Second, the superaggressive expenditure plans have significant variation in prices moving forward. This occurs for two reasons:
  - There is considerable overshooting in the adjustment of the construction labor supply so that it initially increases, but prices drop, causing workers to go to the other, non-construction sectors for employment. This is a result of the transition dynamics assumed for capital and labor adjustments and not the underlying CGE model. That is, the supply elasticities are large enough together with changes in local wages to move workers in and out of the construction labor market.
  - In addition, the use of an eighth-order polynomial to smooth the results did not contribute to this overshooting in the estimates but is part of the raw results.

As Figure 6.1 shows, the results (excluding the superaggressive scenario) suggest that wages were likely to rise on the order of 15 to 25 percent in the first few years from 2019 wages but were likely to fall after that as the labor market adjusts. Wages were likely to return to presurge levels in approximately five to seven years for these three sets of simulations. For the superaggressive set of expenditures, wages during the initial surge could rise as high as

35 to 40 percent, depending on how aggressive expenditures are in the first two years. Wages under the superaggressive expenditure plans will fall back to presurge levels rapidly because total expenditures are likely to reach the full PA allocation.

Equipment

Like in the findings for wages, equipment rental prices were likely to increase in the first few years of rebuilding. Figure 6.2 provides the estimated rental prices for equipment.

The baseline and unconstrained expenditure plans suggest that rental prices were likely to increase on the order of 10 to 15 percent in the first few years of PA expenditures, with a return to near-presurge levels over a longer time horizon than that for wages.

With the aggressive plan, equipment rental prices were likely to increase more in the early years but return to 2019 price levels in less time than for the baseline and unconstrained expenditure plans. There is an inherent trade-off between increasing prices more in the early years and having a longer adjustment period.

As plans become more aggressive, they tend to increase prices early but lower prices more quickly because less work is needed in later years. As a caveat to the equipment analysis, we note that the present model assumes perfect substitutability of equipment across all sectors—both construction and nonconstruction. This assumption mitigates some of the effects of increased construction output because capital can respond flexibly.

FIGURE 6.2
Equipment Rental Prices for Public Assistance Projects

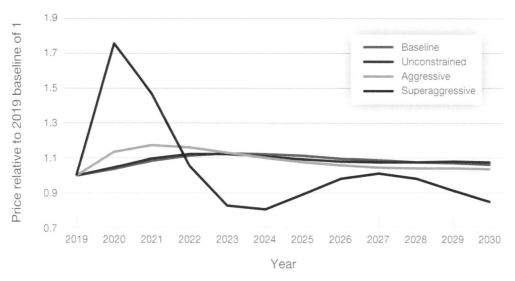

NOTE: The figure shows estimated average equipment rental prices across the sets of expenditure plans. Prices are relative to a baseline price in 2019 of 1.

Materials

The results for material prices are fundamentally different from those for labor and equipment prices. Labor comes from the stock of labor in the labor force, and equipment comes from the stock of equipment in Puerto Rico. Because equipment is a durable good that can be used in a variety of applications across multiple projects, prices might take longer to adjust. This situation is similar to that for labor, in that labor participation and movement from the nonconstruction sector occur over time. Because Puerto Rico is a small, open economy with significant port capacity (including both the Port of San Juan and the Port of Ponce), increasing demand for materials will likely be met by direct material importation at world market prices. Given the modeling assumption of an open economy, we would not expect material prices to rise significantly. Frictions could exist within the market for materials. We consider those in Chapter Seven.

Figure 6.3 provides the results for material prices across all sets of expenditure plans. With the exception of price changes in the superaggressive expenditure plan, material prices are likely to increase only approximately 1 percent. In the superaggressive set of expenditure plans, imports become a barrier and prices rise considerably—on the order of 8 percent during the initial surge of expenditures—but fall back to near unity quickly.

FIGURE 6.3

Material Prices for Public Assistance Projects

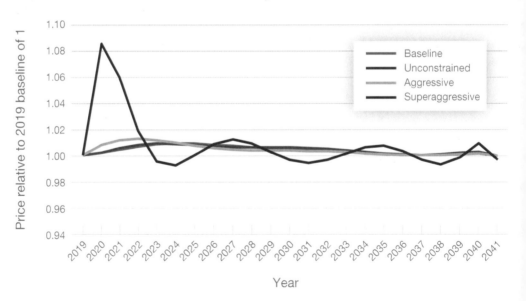

NOTE: The figure shows estimated average material prices across the sets of expenditure plans. Prices are relative to a baseline price in 2019 of 1.

CHAPTER SEVEN

Implementation

Our ultimate goal of this entire project was to provide cost estimators in Puerto Rico some multiplicative factors to modify their cost estimates of future projects to reflect future conditions, taking into account the entire recovery effort. The preceding chapters inform us about these potential factors for labor, materials, and equipment, but only partially:

- First, supply chain frictions are likely to arise early in the reconstruction process, especially with regard to material flows from outside sources. This is because, although there appears to be enough port capacity and warehouse space, the volume of imports is likely to be larger and of a different mix of goods than the current set of imports, which will require hiring and training workers and developing new distribution networks for new goods. Over time, these logistical frictions will be reduced.
- Second, the CGE model does not take into account construction labor in the most appropriate manner for doing cost estimates because construction is, by definition, local but the CGE produces a significant amount of imported construction. We used the results of the CGE together with the analysis described in Chapter Two for labor demands and labor force size to modify the calculations.
- Third, there could be a desire to have a single factor, rather than three separate factors, that applies to the entire project. Although we do not advocate for this approach because of the differences in intensities of the labor, materials, and equipment, we provide it as an option for when the component parts cannot be broken out.

Importantly, cost estimators using the CEF need to know which year on the FPF curve to choose for each of the cost components. In this chapter, we first discuss the selection of the appropriate year. We then discuss how to operationalize the model results for each of the components in turn.

Choosing a Time Point on the Curve

To choose the appropriate escalation factor (Part E), the cost estimator must know the midpoint of the project spending. That is, the estimator locates the midpoint of the expenditure for a project and chooses the point on the corresponding curve for the component. To minimize estimator confusion, we also used the midpoint to choose a point on the FPF curves.

Operationalizing the Model Results for Each Component

Equipment

The equipment FPF is the most straightforward to implement. The FPF for equipment should be thought of as simply another factor that needs to be applied to the Part A estimates of the FEMA CEF. Our FPF curve for equipment is simply the result of the model for equipment prices. We used the fitted average values of the baseline scenario as our best estimate of the real price increases of equipment from 2019 prices.[1] Given the current trajectory of work, combined with knowledge about previous hurricanes that were category 3 or larger, our estimates for the equipment FPF will be equal to the baseline scenario simulations of expenditure plans. The resulting FPF factor should be applied to Part A as a multiplicative factor for equipment costs in the CEF. Table 7.1 provides these estimates for fiscal years 2020 through 2025, which are consistent with the results in Figure 6.2 in Chapter Six, and provides both the mean estimate and the 90-percent confidence interval.

Materials

As a starting point, Table 7.2 provides the point estimates directly from the model, which have been smoothed using the eighth-order polynomial as displayed in Figure 6.3 in Chapter Six for the baseline scenario. In addition, we provide the 5th and 95th percentiles from the 100 stochastic expenditure draws for the baseline scenario.

TABLE 7.1

Estimated Future Price Forecast Factors for Equipment

	Estimated Equipment FPF	
Year	Estimate	5th and 95th Percentiles
2020	1.037	[1.023, 1.088]
2021	1.082	[1.018, 1.097]
2022	1.113	[1.042, 1.144]
2023	1.125	[1.045, 1.200]
2024	1.122	[1.070, 1.211]
2025	1.111	[1.038, 1.197]

NOTE: Equipment FPFs are derived from modeled results using the baseline expenditure plan simulations. These should be applied to Part A estimates in a multiplicative fashion.

---

[1] We used only the baseline scenario rather than the range of potential scenarios because the baseline was the least aggressive scenario and, for 2018 to 2020, we saw little movement in the construction sector in Puerto Rico that would reflect aggressive investment.

TABLE 7.2

Estimated Future Price Forecasts for Materials

Year	Estimated Material FPF	
	Estimate	5th and 95th Percentiles
2020	1.003	[1.001, 1.004]
2021	1.004	[1.001, 1.006]
2022	1.006	[1.002, 1.009]
2023	1.008	[1.003, 1.013]
2024	1.009	[1.004, 1.013]
2025	1.007	[1.003, 1.013]

NOTE: Material FPFs are derived from modeled results using the baseline expenditure plan simulations.

In 2016, Puerto Rico imported about $24 billion in merchandise from CONUS and approximately $19 billion from foreign sources (Puerto Rico Planning Board, 2017). These values suggest that more than half the imports to Puerto Rico are from CONUS but that there are significant imports from the rest of the world. This pattern is consistent with a small, open economy near a large economy with a common currency (see, for example, Ivus and Strong, 2007, p. 44). Given the size of the overall U.S. economy and its proximity, we would expect there to be considerable imports from CONUS. This also suggests that CONUS-based supply chains might be stressed as work ramps up, and this possibility is not incorporated into the model. If we can judge from previous natural disaster recovery efforts, material prices have risen on the order of 10 percent in the immediate ramp-up of construction efforts, although the literature suggests that these increases could be as high as 20 to 25 percent (see Gyourko and Saiz, 2004; Gyourko and Saiz, 2006; A. Murphy, 2018; Olsen and Porter, 2011; and Somerville, 1999). Although we believe that prices are not likely to spike considerably, there could be frictions that are not incorporated into the model. The model predicts that material prices are likely to rise only 1 to 2 percent in the first years of reconstruction efforts. For this report, we therefore conservatively assumed that 2020 material prices were likely to be 10 percent higher than 2019 prices, with a linear decline over the subsequent five years. Table 7.3 provides the material FPF factors for fiscal years 2020 through 2025.

Labor

As a starting point, Table 7.4 provides the point estimates directly from the model, smoothed using the eighth-order polynomial as displayed in Figure 6.1 for wages in Chapter Six. In addition, we provide the 5th and 95th percentiles from the 100 stochastic expenditure draws from the baseline scenario.

TABLE 7.3

Estimated Future Price Forecast Factors for Materials

Year	Estimated Material FPF
2020	1.10
2021	1.08
2022	1.06
2023	1.04
2024	1.02
2025	1.00

NOTE: Material FPF factors are based on modeled results together with a recognition that there might be frictions within Puerto Rico's economy that the model did not consider. Modifications to the FPF factors are based on previous literature consistent with an initial spike and mitigation of the spike over a relatively short duration. We provide no confidence interval here because there are likely frictions not accounted for in the model, so we are using our best estimates.

TABLE 7.4

Estimated Future Price Forecasts for Local Labor

Year	Estimated Labor FPF	
	Estimate	5th and 95th Percentiles
2020	1.196	[1.092, 1.240]
2021	1.117	[1.035, 1.156]
2022	1.094	[1.027, 1.140]
2023	1.069	[0.993, 1.139]
2024	1.048	[0.971, 1.158]
2025	0.920	[0.792, 0.986]

NOTE: Labor FPFs are derived from modeled results using the baseline expenditure plan simulations and are for local labor only.

As discussed previously, there is likely to be a mismatch between the skills necessary to complete the recovery efforts and the labor available locally. Our occupational analysis described in Chapter Two suggests not only that a considerable expansion of the labor force will be needed to meet even a moderate expenditure plan consistent with the baseline but that some skills might not be present in Puerto Rico's local labor force. At a minimum, approximately 50 percent of the labor for the construction recovery is likely to come from CONUS. If more-aggressive expenditure plans are implemented, this proportion is likely to rise. Even with the baseline scenario, informed by previous emergency recovery efforts, the analysis in Chapter Two, and results from the CGE suggesting that approximately 70 to 80 percent of construction would be imported, we estimated that approximately 75 percent of the recovery labor needs would be filled by CONUS sources.

Our economywide model estimates only the local wages and not those derived from nonlocal sources. As a result, the model output needs to be modified to be consistent with the multiple sources of labor needed to carry out the recovery construction efforts. We followed previous efforts to create a weighted average of local and CONUS-based labor forces. Our estimates from the economywide model were used to modify the local wages moving forward and averaged with CONUS-based labor that is paid a premium for working in Puerto Rico and a per diem rate. Our estimates of a 25-percent wage premium were consistent with previous efforts.

To estimate the per diem rate, we assumed the federal per diem rate but also double occupancy of hotels, so that the lodging rate was half of the federal lodging rate, but the rates for dining and incidentals remained at the federal levels. For Puerto Rico, this results in a 25-percent per diem rate for the national average construction salary with a 25-percent wage premium.

Further, our results are in real terms, and the Puerto Rico recovery is not likely to increase construction wages in CONUS. Cost estimators for FEMA use Gordian's RSMeans software to estimate the cost of projects. RSMeans provides estimates across most locations in the United States. The city cost index (CCI) for each location allows national average costs to be estimated in local areas. Baseline national average construction wages are set to unity, and the CCI allows the translation of national average wages to local wages. For example, if wages in Puerto Rico were 0.28, wages in Puerto Rico would be 28 percent of national average wages.

Gordian has developed a set of three CCIs for Puerto Rico: urban, rural, and remote islands. For expositional simplicity, we refer to them as CCI_{labor}, recognizing that there are multiple zones within Puerto Rico. To estimate the FPF for labor, we first needed to estimate the future price of labor based on a weighted average of local future prices and CONUS prices. The formula for the future price of labor is given by Equation 7.1:

$$P_{labor} = 0.25 * CCI_{labor} * FPF_{labor} + 0.75 * \text{wage premium} * \text{per diem}. \tag{7.1}$$

Based on the economywide model, FPFs for local labor are given in Table 7.5. Gordian's estimates for the zonal CCI are given in Table 7.6.

As an example, to estimate the future price relative to national average prices for zone 1 in 2020, we would calculate

$$FPF_{1,2020} = 0.25 * 0.318 * 1.152 + 0.75 * 1.25 * 1.25 = 1.263. \tag{7.2}$$

CEF Part A uses RSMeans wages that contain the appropriate CCI adjustment. These wages are then adjusted using a multiplicative factor to reflect the FPF. To calculate this multiplicative factor using Puerto Rico prices as a baseline, we therefore needed to divide the local wage by the CCI. In the example above, we divided the future price of labor (1.263) by

TABLE 7.5

Future Price Forecasts for Labor

Year	FPF for Local Labor
2020	1.152
2021	1.157
2022	1.112
2023	1.065
2024	1.033
2025	1.019

TABLE 7.6

Gordian Labor City Cost Indexes for Puerto Rico for 2019

Zone	Labor CCI
1: urban	0.318
2: rural	0.312
3: remote islands	0.463

SOURCE: Gordian RSMeans data provided to the authors.

the zone 1 (urban) labor CCI (0.318) and obtained a factor of 3.973. Table 7.7 provides the labor multiplicative factors by zone and year.

A Single Future Price Forecast Factor for Square-Footage Estimates

In some cases, square-footage estimates were used to estimate the cost of construction. In such cases, modifying costs by individual component factors might not be feasible. To address this case, we estimated single adjustment factors for entire construction costs. To estimate such a single factor, given the multiple sources of labor, we needed to find the future price of

TABLE 7.7

Future Price Forecast Labor Factors for Puerto Rico, by Zone and Year

Zone	2020	2021	2022	2023	2024	2025
1: urban	3.973	3.974	3.963	3.951	3.943	3.940
2: rural	4.044	4.045	4.034	4.022	4.014	4.010
3: remote islands	2.819	2.820	2.809	2.797	2.790	2.786

NOTE: Multiplicative factors for labor for use on Part A of the CEF labor costs are defined by zone by year.

completing a construction project and divide it by the current price of completing the project to produce a multiplicative factor for the FPF. Gordian has provided the current price of all components by zone; these are reproduced in Table 7.8.

We used these estimates together with an assumption that all of Gordian's data were based on local markets. In particular, we assumed that there was no CONUS labor included in the CCI. We then estimated the current cost of construction based on the average construction cost breakdowns for buildings in the RSMeans data. These estimates are 37 percent of costs from labor, 5 percent from equipment, and 58 percent from materials. Table 7.9 provides our estimates of current construction costs where the baseline national average cost is unity.

Next, using the same method, we used the estimated future prices determined by the FPF components to estimate future prices for entire construction costs: We applied the relative cost weights to each of the FPF components and combined them. Table 7.10 provides the estimated future costs.

Finally, we took the ratio of the entries in Table 7.10 to those in Table 7.9 to obtain single-factor FPF factors in Table 7.11.

TABLE 7.8
City Cost Indexes for Puerto Rico, by Zone and Component, 2019

Zone	Labor CCI	Material CCI	Equipment CCI
1: urban	0.318	1.254	0.998
2: rural	0.312	1.316	0.998
3: remote islands	0.463	1.451	0.998

SOURCE: Gordian data provided to the authors.

TABLE 7.9
Current Cost of Construction, by Zone

Zone	Current Cost of Construction
1: urban	0.88552
2: rural	0.91858
3: remote islands	1.05291

TABLE 7.10
Future Costs of Entire Construction

Zone	2020	2021	2022	2023	2024	2025
1: urban	1.318	1.306	1.292	1.277	1.262	1.246
2: rural	1.356	1.344	1.329	1.313	1.297	1.281
3: remote islands	1.457	1.443	1.426	1.408	1.390	1.373

TABLE 7.11

Single-Factor Future Price Forecast Factors for Use with Square-Footage Estimates

Zone	2020	2021	2022	2023	2024	2025
1: urban	1.489	1.475	1.459	1.442	1.425	1.407
2: rural	1.477	1.463	1.447	1.430	1.412	1.395
3: remote islands	1.384	1.371	1.355	1.338	1.320	1.304

NOTE: Multiplicative factors for square-footage estimator for use on Part A of CEF costs are defined by zone by year.

Implications

These results suggest that, if construction had begun on the approximately $2.9 billion in obligated PA construction as of late 2019, future prices for this work in 2020 would be approximately 38 to 51 percent higher than for construction completed in 2019 (FEMA, 2021b). These estimates were designed for use in costing PA recovery efforts in Puerto Rico following Hurricane María and were based on an economywide model and forecasted through 2025. Estimates were provided for each of the main cost components of PA work: labor, materials, and equipment. We recommend that the labor, material, and equipment factors be used whenever possible.

We note that all estimates are in *real* 2019 dollars, implying that *inflation will further raise nominal expenditures in the future*. Additionally, we note that the factors were designed to be used in conjunction with 2019 RSMeans prices. Because quarterly price updates from Gordian reflect price increases (because of surging demand), the FPF will have to be revised downward to prevent double-counting because the prices from Gordian will embody some of the FPFs because the FPFs were based on 2019 prices and cost estimators were using then-current prices.

Labor costs are likely to increase owing to the lack of available skilled labor in Puerto Rico and the consequent importation of CONUS-based labor. We estimated that Puerto Rico–based labor would increase by nearly 16 percent in the early phases of reconstruction; labor costs would lessen over the recovery as markets adjust to the new equilibrium, although there is likely to be considerable imported labor because of the skill mix necessary for the recovery efforts.

Equipment costs are likely to grow during the reconstruction efforts. This growth is due to the increase in labor costs and substitutability of equipment for laborers as labor costs increase. The lag in equipment price increases is largely due to delays in equipment importation and the lack of service infrastructure for maintenance.

CHAPTER EIGHT

Discussion and Limitations

The most important set of assumptions in this analysis, and the one that is most likely to be incorrect, is the expenditure path. We have used historical FEMA obligations as a guide to the development of the expenditure path, as well as additional assumptions about the likely pace of spending given the amount and types of storm damage. Given the critical importance of the pace of spending, rather than rely on a single expenditure path, we incorporated a stochastic process to develop *a set of potential expenditure paths*. This resulted in a variety of FPF curves that could be used as the factors for adjusting the Part A cost estimates. If the historical data were not representative of the situation in Puerto Rico, our estimates will, by definition, be off.

To update the forecasts and benchmark them to what is happening in Puerto Rico, we recommend that the on-the-ground prices be monitored by triangulating from three sources:

- First, Gordian provides the underlying data for the cost estimates, and these should be included in any monitoring effort. As prices rise because of increased construction activities, these increases will be incorporated in local prices for labor, materials, and equipment. The FPF incorporates this increase in prices and, if not modified to reflect increases in on-the-ground prices, the combined CEF will double-count price increases: once in the actual price increases and a second time for the anticipated increase. Current FPF estimates are based on 2019 prices, while cost estimators tend to use the most-recent prices available; consequently, there could already be some double-counting if this discrepancy is not taken into account. FPF curves should be reduced if there are significant increases in price that the FPF incorporates. This should be monitored quarterly and the FPF reduced when the difference between estimated prices and current prices is greater than 10 percent.
- Second, BLS provides information on wages and employment at the territory, sector, and occupation levels at varying temporal lags. Importantly, the BLS data are worksite-level data (rather than just local contractors, which are the source of the Gordian data). If local contractors employ CONUS-based labor, these results might not hold going forward. As a result, significant increases in higher-wage CONUS labor in Puerto Rico will be reflected in the BLS data but might not be captured in the Gordian data. By using prehurricane BLS data together with Gordian's wage data, we can better understand the labor mix of local and imported that is being used in Puerto Rico as the recovery

takes place. Additionally, BLS employment data will allow monitoring, with only a one-month lag, the level of construction employment. This reveals when increases in construction output are taking place and when to mark to market the expenditure curves so that they represent what is actually taking place on the ground in Puerto Rico.

- Third, Puerto Rico's Economic Development Bank collects data on a variety of economic indicators. Of special interest to this work is its collection of near-real-time sales of cement. Because much of the construction in Puerto Rico uses concrete, this provides a means of proxying for construction-related activities. Taken together, these data provide information about the speed and scale of PA-related activities that will allow updating the FPF curves, as well as understanding of how expenditures are taking place.

The Gordian price and wage data are updated quarterly; some of the BLS data are updated monthly, while other data series are quarterly, with a lag; and the Economic Development Bank data are updated monthly. Thus, we recommend quarterly updates to the FPFs. Because there is currently an error allowance within the CEF of up to 10 percent, we suggest that, when the deviation between the estimated future costs (FPF estimates) and actual costs are greater than 10 percent, an update is warranted. This would affect projects that have not received cost estimates and would not be a redo of previous cost estimates. This will help avoid double-counting, as mentioned earlier. Additionally, if actual expenditures are not consistent with our estimated PA expenditures, this can be accounted for in FPF updates. This would not allow a redo of previous estimates, but the main hope is to avoid overestimates in which Gordian prices reflect the estimates of price increases.

Because different types of projects require different mixes of labor, materials, and equipment, we advise FEMA to use the individual factor FPFs whenever possible rather than the single factor. Our estimates for the single factor are based on the "average" relative mix of labor, materials, and equipment for a small selection of typical buildings, which is considerably different from other types of infrastructure construction, such as roads, bridges, water, and power.

The methods described in this report can be readily adapted to other areas of the United States that have experienced large-scale natural disasters because the data come from sources that have nationwide coverage. Importantly, a combination of the occupational analysis presented in Chapter Two and a calibration of the CGE model described in Chapter Four could be used to determine the need for an FPF. From our perspective, the labor component could be the most important component in determining whether an FPF would be necessary for a specific community. Markets for materials and equipment can readily respond to market incentives, but labor is a more complex case because the need for housing and other supports might not be met in the short term for damaged communities. For most communities in the United States, the flow of labor will ultimately respond to normal market incentives. In communities that are particularly isolated, such as Puerto Rico and the U.S. Virgin Islands, considerable investment must be taken to travel to those areas that would need to be compensated so that skilled labor is available. Finally, the skill mix of labor could be a critically important a factor in the recovery efforts because, even if there is enough labor, workers might not have the skills necessary to complete a large-scale effort, especially for infrastructure, such as electricity and water.

From our perspective, the need for an FPF is likely to be uncommon but possible; this is because most markets in the United States are well integrated and highly efficient. The combination of a large-scale event, relative to the size of the economy, and a relatively isolated market are likely to produce a situation in which an FPF might be necessary, as was the case with Puerto Rico and the U.S. Virgin Islands. Many factors can cause building and infrastructure prices to rise—disruptions in trade, labor strikes, worldwide pandemic, or macroeconomic policy—that are outside of the scope of the current work and are not taken into consideration in generating an FPF.

Abbreviations

BEA	Bureau of Economic Analysis
BLS	U.S. Bureau of Labor Statistics
CCI	city cost index
CEF	Cost Estimating Format
CES	constant elasticity of substitution
CGE	computable general equilibrium
COA	course of action
CONUS	continental United States
CPS	Current Population Survey
EMMIE	Emergency Management Mission Integrated Environment
FEMA	Federal Emergency Management Agency
FPF	future price forecast
GDP	gross domestic product
NAICS	North American Industry Classification System
PA	Public Assistance
SAM	Social Accounting Matrix
SOC	Standard Occupational Classification

Bibliography

BLS—*See* U.S. Bureau of Labor Statistics.

Bond, Craig A., Aaron Strong, Troy D. Smith, Megan Andrew, John S. Crown, Kathryn A. Edwards, Gabriella C. Gonzalez, Italo A. Gutierrez, Lauren Kendrick, Jill E. Luoto, Kyle Pratt, Karishma Patel, Alexander D. Rothenberg, Mark Stalczynski, Patricia K. Tong, and Melanie A. Zaber, *Challenges and Opportunities for the Puerto Rico Economy: A Review of Evidence and Options Following Hurricanes Irma and Maria in 2017,* Homeland Security Operational Analysis Center operated by the RAND Corporation, RR-2600-DHS, 2020. As of October 11, 2021: https://www.rand.org/pubs/research_reports/RR2600.html

Bureau of Economic Analysis, U.S. Department of Commerce, "Gross Domestic Product for Puerto Rico, 2019: First Official Release of GDP for Puerto Rico, 2012–2019," news release BEA 21-45, September 27, 2021. As of October 17, 2021: https://www.bea.gov/news/2021/gross-domestic-product-puerto-rico-2019

Capen, E. C., R. V. Clapp, and W. M. Campbell, "Competitive Bidding in High-Risk Situations," *Journal of Petroleum Technology*, Vol. 23, No. 6, June 1, 1971, pp. 641–653.

Card, David, and Thomas Lemieux, "Can Falling Supply Explain the Rising Return to College for Younger Men? A Cohort-Based Analysis," *Quarterly Journal of Economics*, Vol. 116, No. 2, May 2001, pp. 705–746.

Central Office for Recovery, Reconstruction and Resiliency, *Transformation and Innovation in the Wake of Devastation: An Economic and Disaster Recovery Plan for Puerto Rico*, August 8, 2018. As of November 17, 2021: https://reliefweb.int/report/puerto-rico-united-states-america/ transformation-and-innovation-wake-devastation-economic-and

Chetty, Raj, "Bounds on Elasticities with Optimization Frictions: A Synthesis of Micro and Macro Evidence on Labor Supply," *Econometrica*, Vol. 80, No. 3, May 2012, pp. 969–1018.

Echenique, Martin, and Luis Melgar, "Mapping Puerto Rico's Hurricane Migration with Mobile Phone Data," CityLab, May 11, 2018. As of October 17, 2021: https://www.bloomberg.com/news/articles/2018-05-11/ where-puerto-rico-s-residents-migrated-since-maria

Federal Emergency Management Agency, U.S. Department of Homeland Security, *Public Assistance Alternative Procedures (Section 428): Guide for Permanent Work FEMA-4339-DR-PR,* February 10, 2020. As of October 17, 2021: https://recovery.pr/documents/ PAAP_Guide_for_Permanent_Work_DR_4339_PR_V3_2_10_2020_FINAL_508.pdf

———, "Program Overview," webpage, last updated May 6, 2021a. As of October 17, 2021: https://www.fema.gov/assistance/public/program-overview

———, "OpenFEMA Dataset: Public Assistance Funded Projects Details—v1," webpage, last data refresh November 16, 2021b. As of October 13, 2021: https://www.fema.gov/openfema-data-page/public-assistance-funded-projects-details-v1

Federal Reserve Bank of St. Louis, "Gross Domestic Product for Puerto Rico (NYGDPMKTPCDPRI)," webpage, updated July 1, 2021. As of October 17, 2021: https://fred.stlouisfed.org/series/NYGDPMKTPCDPRI

FEMA—*See* Federal Emergency Management Agency.

Gonzalez, Gabriella C., Kathryn A. Edwards, Melanie A. Zaber, Megan Andrew, Aaron Strong, and Craig A. Bond, *Supporting a 21st Century Workforce in Puerto Rico: Challenges and Options for Improving Puerto Rico's Workforce System Following Hurricanes Irma and Maria in 2017*, Homeland Security Operational Analysis Center operated by the RAND Corporation, RR-2856-DHS, 2020. As of October 11, 2021:
https://www.rand.org/pubs/research_reports/RR2856.html

Goolsbee, Austan, "Investment Tax Incentives, Prices, and the Supply of Capital Goods," *Quarterly Journal of Economics*, Vol. 113, No. 1, February 1998, pp. 121–148.

Governor's 2018 recovery plan—*See* Central Office for Recovery, Reconstruction and Resiliency, 2018.

Granger, Clive W. J., "Can We Improve the Perceived Quality of Economic Forecasts?" *Journal of Applied Econometrics*, Vol. 11, No. 5, September–October 1996, pp. 455–473.

Gyourko, Joseph, and Albert Saiz, "Reinvestment in the Housing Stock: The Role of Construction Costs and the Supply Side," *Journal of Urban Economics*, Vol. 55, No. 2, March 2004, pp. 238–256.

———, "Construction Costs and the Supply of Housing Structure," *Journal of Regional Science*, Vol. 46, No. 4, October 2006, pp. 661–680.

Hinojosa, Jennifer, and Edwin Meléndez, "Puerto Rican Exodus: One Year Since Hurricane Maria," City University of New York, Hunter College, Center for Puerto Rican Studies, Research Brief 2018-05, September 2018. As of January 15, 2019:
https://centropr.hunter.cuny.edu/research/data-center/research-briefs/puerto-rican-exodus-one-year-hurricane-maria

IMPLAN, homepage, undated. As of October 12, 2021:
https://www.implan.com/

Ivus, Olena, and Aaron Strong, "Modeling Approaches to the Analysis of Trade Policy: Computable General Equilibrium and Gravity Models," in William A. Kerr and James D. Gaisford, eds., *Handbook on International Trade Policy*, Northampton, Mass.: Edward Elgar, 2007, pp. 44–56.

Katz, Lawrence F., and Kevin M. Murphy, "Changes in Relative Wages, 1963–1987: Supply and Demand Factors," *Quarterly Journal of Economics*, Vol. 107, No. 1, February 1992, pp. 35–78.

Lamba-Nieves, Deepak, and Raúl Santiago-Bartolomei, "Transforming the Recovery into Locally-Led Growth: Federal Contracting in the Post-Disaster Period," Center for the New Economy, September 26, 2018. As of October 17, 2021:
https://grupocne.org/2018/09/26/transforming-the-recovery-into-locally-led-growth-federal-contracting-in-the-post-disaster-period/

McClelland, Robert, and Shannon Mok, *A Review of Recent Research on Labor Supply Elasticities*, Washington, D.C.: Congressional Budget Office, Working Paper 2012-12, October 25, 2012. As of October 11, 2021:
https://www.cbo.gov/publication/43675

Milligan, Susan, "The Skilled Worker Exodus," *U.S. News and World Report*, May 11, 2018. As of October 17, 2021:
https://www.usnews.com/news/the-report/articles/2018-05-11/skilled-workers-are-leaving-puerto-rico-in-droves

Murphy, Alvin, "A Dynamic Model of Housing Supply," *American Economic Journal: Economic Policy*, Vol. 10, No. 4, November 2018, pp. 243–267.

Murphy, Kevin M., and Finis Welch, "The Structure of Wages," *Quarterly Journal of Economics*, Vol. 107, No. 1, February 1992, pp. 285–326.

MyLifeElsewhere, "Cost of Living Comparison," webpage, undated. As of March 15, 2019: https://www.mylifeelsewhere.com/cost-of-living/united-states/puerto-rico

Nadreau, Timothy P., "WSU CGE Analysis of Carbon WA: Technical Documentation," *Western Economics Forum*, Vol. 14, No. 2, Fall 2015, pp. 26–56. As of October 11, 2021: https://waeaonline.org/western_econ_forum/ wsu-cge-analysis-of-carbon-wa-technical-documentation/

Olsen, Anna H., and Keith A. Porter, *On the Contribution of Reconstruction Labor Wages and Material Prices to Demand Surge*, University of Colorado, Boulder, Department of Civil Environmental and Architectural Engineering, Structural Engineering and Structural Mechanics 11-1, August 2011. As of October 11, 2021: https://pubs.er.usgs.gov/publication/70045146

Perroni, Carlo, and Thomas F. Rutherford, "Regular Flexibility of Nested CES Functions," *European Economic Review*, Vol. 39, No. 2, February 1995, pp. 335–343.

Public Law 71-798, an act relating to the rate of wages for laborers and mechanics employed on public buildings of the United States and the District of Columbia by contractors and subcontractors, and for other purposes, March 3, 1931. As of November 17, 2021: https://govtrackus.s3.amazonaws.com/legislink/pdf/stat/46/STATUTE-46-Pg1494.pdf

Public Law 93-288, Disaster Relief Act of 1974, May 22, 1974. As of November 7, 2020: https://www.hsdl.org/?abstract&did=458661

Public Law 107-296, Homeland Security Act of 2002, November 25, 2002. As of May 12, 2019: https://www.govinfo.gov/app/details/PLAW-107publ296

Public Law 113-2, An act making supplemental appropriations for the fiscal year ending September 30, 2013, to improve and streamline disaster assistance for Hurricane Sandy, and for other purposes, January 29, 2013. As of November 7, 2020: https://www.govinfo.gov/app/details/PLAW-113publ2

Puerto Rico Planning Board, Office of the Governor, *Puerto Rico External Trade Statistics 2016*, February 2017.

Rausch, Sebastian, and Thomas F. Rutherford, *Tools for Building National Economic Models Using State-Level IMPLAN Social Accounts*, July 2008. As of January 15, 2019: http://www.mpsge.org/IMPLAN2006inGAMS/IMPLAN2006inGAMS.pdf

Rutherford, Thomas F., and Andrew Schreiber, "blueNOTE: National Open Source Tools for General Equilibrium Analysis," University of Wisconsin–Madison, College of Agricultural and Life Sciences; Wisconsin Institute for Discovery at the University of Wisconsin–Madison; and Environmental Defense Fund, undated. As of October 13, 2021: https://aae.wisc.edu/blueNOTE/

Sandy Recovery Improvement Act—*See* Public Law 113-2.

Somerville, C. Tsuriel, "Residential Construction Costs and the Supply of New Housing: Endogeneity and Bias in Construction Cost Indexes," *Journal of Real Estate Finance and Economics*, Vol. 18, No. 1, 1999, pp. 43–62.

Strong, Aaron, Jeffrey B. Wenger, Drew M. Anderson, Kathryn A. Edwards, and Kyle Siler-Evans, *Review and Validation of a FEMA Methodology: Future Price Forecast for Puerto Rico*, Homeland Security Operational Analysis Center operated by the RAND Corporation, unpublished.

Sue Wing, Ian, *The Regional Impacts of U.S. Climate Change Policy: A General Equilibrium Analysis*, February 27, 2007. As of January 15, 2019:
http://people.bu.edu/isw/papers/burgess_ecomod.pdf

Theil, Henri, *Economic Forecasts and Policy*, Amsterdam: North-Holland, 1961.

U.S. Bureau of Labor Statistics, U.S. Department of Labor, "Economy at a Glance: Puerto Rico," webpage, undated a. As of October 17, 2021:
https://www.bls.gov/eag/eag.pr.htm

———, "Occupational Employment and Wage Statistics," webpage, undated b. As of October 17, 2021:
https://www.bls.gov/oes/

———, "Quarterly Census of Employment and Wages," webpage, last modified August 16, 2019. As of November 18, 2021:
https://www.bls.gov/cew/data.htm

———, "Employment Projections: Industry–Occupation Matrix Data, by Industry," webpage, last modified September 8, 2021. As of October 17, 2021:
https://www.bls.gov/emp/tables/industry-occupation-matrix-industry.htm

U.S. Census Bureau, "Current Population Survey Datasets," webpage, undated. As of October 17, 2021:
https://www.census.gov/programs-surveys/cps/data/datasets.html

U.S. Code, Title 6, Domestic Security; Chapter 1, Homeland Security Organization; Subchapter III, Science and Technology in Support of Homeland Security; Section 185, Federally Funded Research and Development Centers. As of March 20, 2021:
https://uscode.house.gov/view.xhtml?req=(title:6%20section:185%20edition:prelim)

———, Title 42, The Public Health and Welfare; Chapter 68, Disaster Relief; Subchapter IV, Major Disaster Assistance Programs, Section 5189f, Public Assistance Program Alternative Procedures. As of November 7, 2020:
https://uscode.house.gov/view.xhtml?req=(title:42%20section:5189f%20edition:prelim)

Varian, Hal R., *Microeconomic Analysis*, New York: W. W. Norton, 1992.

World Bank, "Population, Total for Puerto Rico," Federal Reserve Bank of St. Louis, webpage, October 15, 2021. Address not available.